M A K I N G
DIVERSITY
H A P P E N

Controversies and Solutions

The Center for Creative Leadership would
like to thank the following organizations
for their generous support of the conference
and research that lead to the publication of
of this book:

Ciba Agricultural Group

The Goodyear Tire & Rubber Company

Sara Lee Corporation

M A K I N G
DIVERSITY
H A P P E N

Controversies and Solutions

Ann M. Morrison
Marian N. Ruderman
Martha Hughes-James

Center for Creative Leadership
Greensboro, North Carolina

The Center for Creative Leadership is an international, nonprofit educational institution founded in 1970 to foster creative leadership and effective management for the good of society overall. As a part of this mission, it publishes books and reports that aim to contribute to a general process of inquiry and understanding in which ideas related to leadership are raised, exchanged, and evaluated. The ideas presented in its publications are those of the author or authors.

The Center thanks you for supporting its work through the purchase of this volume. If you have comments, suggestions, or questions about any Center publication, please contact Bill Drath, Publication Director, at the address given below.

Center for Creative Leadership
Post Office Box 26300
Greensboro, North Carolina 27438-6300

CCL No. 320

Library of Congress Cataloging-in-Publication Data

Making diversity happen : controversies and solutions / Ann M. Morrison, Marian N.
   Ruderman, Martha Hughes-James.
        p.   cm.
     Proceedings of the conference "Leadership diversity: Beyond awareness into action,"
   held in December 1992 at the Center for Creative Leadership in Greensboro, North
   Carolina.
     Report number 320"—Verso of t.p.
     Includes bibliographical references.
     ISBN 0-912879-72-6 (pbk.) : $20.00
       1. Minorities—Employment—Congresses. 2. Multiculturalism—Congresses.
   I. Morrison, Ann M. II. Ruderman, Marian N. III. Hughes-James, Martha.
   HF5549.5.M5M34   1993
   658.3'041—dc20   93-40166
                                                                              CIP

Table of Contents

Acknowledgments

Acknowledging everyone who contributed to this report is a daunting task. We should start by thanking the many people who helped make the conference, "Leadership Diversity: Beyond Awareness Into Action," held at the Center for Creative Leadership in Greensboro, North Carolina, in December of 1992, an exciting, interactive event and one from which we were able to access the ideas that make up this report.

First and foremost, we'd like to thank the conference participants. They brought with them a wealth of experience and a willingness to share which truly made the conference a forum for learning about organizational practices for developing diversity. A special thank-you goes to the individuals from a variety of organizations and academic disciplines (see Appendix A for their biographies) who acted as resource people during the conference. They led sessions, participated in panels, and responded to challenging questions. Their contributions to the conference are quoted and paraphrased at length in this report. The resource people include: Gloria Bonilla-Santiago, Sunny Bradford, Catherine S. Buntaine, Sandra Carrington, Price M. Cobbs, Dawn M. Cross, Elsie Y. Cross, Bernardo M. Ferdman, William C. Friday, Dana E. Friedman, Kay K. Iwata, Susan E. Jackson, Allen I. Kraut, Ginger Lapid-Bogda, Jack McGrory, Frederick A. Miller, Theodore E. Payne, Danelle Scarborough, Terri Sligh, Derald Wing Sue, and David A. Thomas.

We are also grateful to those who led small-group discussions. These facilitators, most of whom are Center staff or adjuncts (see Appendix A for their titles and affiliations), made it possible for all of us to belong to a small discussion group at some time during the conference, where ideas could be further explored and safely aired. They are: Susan W. Dorn, Diane Ducat, Karen Grabow, Lily M. Kelly-Radford, Carole A. Leland, Karen T. McNeil-Miller, Richard A. Morales, Stella M. Nkomo, Craig S. Smith, Joan C. Tavares, Karen Y. Wilson-Starks, and Randall P. White.

As conference organizers, we were fortunate to have the advice of a strong conference-planning committee. We were ably aided by Kristen Crabtree, Susan Dorn, Bill Drath, Lily Kelly-Radford, Karen McNeil-Miller, Craig Smith, and Walt Tornow, all of the Center for Creative Leadership; Taylor Cox of the University of Michigan; Kay Iwata of K. Iwata Associates; and Stella Nkomo of the University of North Carolina at Charlotte. In addition, Catherine Buntaine of the Kaleel Jamison Consulting Group contributed her expertise to help us design the conference and select people to invite.

Also, Donna Thompson of Baruch College, The City University of New York, co-designed the survey used to collect data from participants before and after the conference.

The hard work of numerous Center staff was invaluable to us when planning the conference and in seeing that it ran smoothly. In particular, we'd like to thank Patti Hall who coordinated our administrative needs for the conference and made sure participants had what they needed when they needed it. Debbie Nelson and Marlene Zagon also provided invaluable administrative support when it came to communicating with the resource people and group facilitators.

Walt Tornow, vice president of research and publication at the Center, acted as our champion and gave us moral and organizational support throughout the planning of the conference and the development of this manuscript.

We would also like to express our appreciation to CIBA Plant Protection; The Goodyear Tire and Rubber Company; and Sara Lee Corporation for their gracious donations in support of the work of this conference. With their gifts we were able to help fund the development of the conference and the publication of this report.

And finally we'd like to thank those who helped us with this report. We are grateful for the comments of Bill Drath, publication director; the editorial advice of Marcia Horowitz and Martin Wilcox; and the assistance of Joanne Ferguson with design and proofreading. We'd also like to acknowledge the contributions of Debbie Nelson and Brian Schrum in the preparation of this manuscript.

Introduction

The Center for Creative Leadership has long had an interest in the issue of diversity in the workplace. It has conducted several studies, including research on the obstacles facing female executives (Morrison, White, & Van Velsor, 1992) and the research for *The New Leaders: Guidelines on Leadership Diversity in America,* which identified the best practices for advancing people of color and white women into senior management (Morrison, 1992). Another expression of this interest was the conference that the Center hosted on December 1, 2, and 3, 1992. Entitled "Leadership Diversity: Beyond Awareness Into Action," it brought together one hundred twenty-two participants with various backgrounds and interests to share ideas on, and experiences with, developing diversity in organizations.

As conference organizers, we wanted to promote interaction and provoke action, and we designed the meeting accordingly. Instead of following a typical format of having a series of lectures in which a few speakers address largely passive audiences, we structured the conference so that everyone would be actively involved in an effort to debate diversity goals and discuss how to implement them. To facilitate the exchange of ideas, we used a variety of formats—concurrent sessions with speakers, a scenario-based panel discussion, interactive theater, small-group discussions, and sessions requested by participants on an ad hoc basis—and we recruited a group of individuals with extensive frontline experience in diversity efforts to act as resource people throughout. (See Appendix A for a full description of how the conference was organized and who the resource people were.)

Our aim for this publication is the same as for the conference, and we have therefore not produced a traditional proceedings. Instead of presenting a session-by-session account of what took place, we offer here chapters on each of four major themes that were sounded throughout the sessions: What does diversity mean to organizations? (chapter 1). How can organizational commitment to diversity be developed? (chapter 2). How should a diversity initiative proceed? (chapter 3). What are some important diversity practices? (chapter 4). We then conclude with a discussion of what the next steps in achieving diversity should be (chapter 5). Thus, this publication is an attempt to synthesize the views of many of today's leading diversity thinkers and practitioners on some key issues related to making diversity happen.

The overall interpretation offered here is, of course, our own. We have, however, tried to be as representative as possible. We identified the four themes after reviewing a great deal of conference data, including audiotapes and videotapes of the sessions; notes from small-group discussions; the results of a preconference poll that asked participants about practices and controversies central to developing a diversity initiative; the responses to a questionnaire administered at the end of the conference which asked participants for their learnings and their plans for next steps; and the results of a postconference poll (sent out two months after the meeting) that repeated many of the questions from the first poll and which asked again about conference learnings and also about action taken since the conference (see Appendix B for copies of the three surveys and summaries of the quantitative data). We refer to this data throughout. In particular, we reguarly quote or paraphrase what participants said, especially the comments of resource people.

The field of diversity today finds itself at a formative moment. After years of effort which naturally concentrated on raising awareness about inequities, it now must find a way to take action to change the policies, attitudes, and conditions that prevented women and people of color from full participation in the workplace. Many of the possible actions are risky—in that they affect a lot of people in important ways—and therefore controversial. In the conference and in this publication we discussed what has been learned about those actions. We believe that it is only by exchanging ideas and experience about diversity practices that we will be able to take the wisest and most effective action.

Chapter 1
WHAT DOES DIVERSITY MEAN TO ORGANIZATIONS?

Diversity is not easy to discuss. The definition of it is still evolving, as is the field devoted to it. When we speak of diversity, are we referring to a work force, including all levels of management, in which the proportions of men and women and ethnic and racial groups are the same as for the population in general? Are there other dimensions of difference that should be included, such as cognitive styles? What aims and methods should the field include? Should action be addressed primarily to the individual, the organization, or society in general?

At many of the conference sessions participants struggled with such questions. In this chapter we will present a synthesis of what the participants had to say about these and related questions.

What Is Diversity?

Diane Ducat, a professor with the City University of New York, referred to the striking level of tension around the question, "What is the problem boundary?" In other words, what is it that we are really trying to change? Ducat observed that there are three areas in which change is often seen as essential:

First, we need to respond to organizational inefficiencies. Some people are motivated to address diversity issues because organizations are losing talent. People of color, white women, and other nontraditional employees are leaving at a faster rate than white male employees. Turnover is costly, and it may reflect inadequate use of the talent available in the work force.

Second, we need to respond to a changing world. The shifting demographics of the labor market and the consumer market have gotten the attention of executives in many organizations. The globalization strategy of organizations also affects their sensitivity to cultural differences and their willingness to make adjustments to be more competitive in the world market.

Third, we need to respond to oppression. Racism and sexism, along with other prejudices, have disadvantaged various groups of people for centuries. A moral imperative requires that organizations take steps to right past wrongs, to make sure that discrimination is eliminated from organizational practices, and to provide opportunities to members of groups that have been oppressed.

The dilemma some see in facing these issues is whether our main goal should be to fix business or to fix the victim. These are not necessarily mutually exclusive, but they do cause some confusion, and sometimes conflict. One skeptical participant, for example, asked, "Am I trying to solve world hunger?" A goal of social responsibility might be construed as interfering with business goals such as productivity. Gloria Bonilla-Santiago, a professor of social work and researcher of issues of Hispanic women and migrant workers, summed up the feeling of some participants: "We went from slavery to segregation, to affirmative action, to diversity. We are looking for ways to define this whole thing that we don't know how to deal with."

Another problem in facing these issues is that different organizations are at different stages of readiness with respect to their views on diversity. Bernardo Ferdman, a researcher, professor, and consultant specializing in workplace and cultural diversity, reflects these stages in the following five approaches to diversity evolution in multinational organizations, which he synthesized and interpreted from models developed in the literature (Adler, 1991; Cox, 1991; Perlmutter, 1969): (1) parochial (Our way is the only way); (2) ethnocentric (Our way is the best way); (3) polycentric (Our way is best for us; their way is best for them); (4) synergistic (Our way and their way differ, and we can learn from each other); and (5) multicultural (There are a multitude of ways, and there are a multitude of best ways; we can learn from and complement one another).

These different stages contribute to the confusion organizations have around understanding diversity issues. Other business problems are not nearly as muddy—speeding up the new-product-development cycle, for example, or improving quality. The fuzziness of the definition and goals of diversity make action difficult. Diane Ducat commented, "It is easy to see why practitioners thus far have tended to engage in a shotgun approach, a scattering of practices."

Despite the problems of definition and evolution, there was some agreement at the conference that the diversity field needs to address three levels: the personal or individual level, the interpersonal or group level, and the organizational or systemic level. At the first level, Price Cobbs, a psychiatrist and management consultant specializing in leadership development and multicultural communications, believes individuals must do some introspection regarding their values. Elsie Cross, an organizational development consultant specializing in diversity interventions, believes that individuals must confront their own and others' behaviors at this level, challenging what others of their group do that perpetuate discrimination.

At the interpersonal level, affiliation patterns are the focus for Cobbs. He finds this level to be challenging because people tend to segregate themselves socially and are consequently more comfortable with others who are like themselves. In fact, he said that many blacks don't want whites in their homes because they fear that if whites see that they have nice accommodations, they will hold that against them. Changing traditional socialization patterns, and creating more diverse work groups, is part of the work at this level.

At the organizational level, diversity needs to be built in as a core value so that the formal and informal business practices support rather than discourage diversity. Cobbs and others noted that until there are diverse success models in an organization, people of color, white women, or anyone else will only be able to get ahead by becoming a clone of somebody. Visible diversity in this case may be only skin deep. Cobbs sees a need for coaches in organizations who will value two-way communication with younger protegés and make an effort to understand and incorporate differences. "What is it like," a coach should ask, "to be twenty-five years old and a Japanese-American with a slight accent in this organization?"

Addressing all three of these levels was recommended by several people at the conference as a way to increase the effectiveness of a diversity initiative. According to Elsie Cross, managing diversity means "ameliorating racism, sexism, heterosexism, ageism, antisemitism, and all other forms of discrimination at the individual, group, and organizational levels." It involves a variety of responsibilities, such as challenging one's own and others' stereotypes and fears, affirming people by giving everyone equal access and attention, utilizing all resources to successfully integrate the organization, and shifting cultural norms and values.

The need to take a comprehensive approach to developing diversity, recognizing that it is a long-term change process, is one area of considerable agreement, even though the definition of diversity may vary from one person and one organization to another. As we will see below, there are disparate views as to whether race and sex play a dominant role in diversity.

Although participants do not agree on most aspects of what constitutes diversity, they do agree that working for it is risky and draining. Ginger Lapid-Bogda, a consultant specializing in large-scale change efforts, building high-performance teams, and diversity, commented:

Doing this work is dangerous. I don't want to underestimate that. It is dangerous. We are walking on the edge. Sometimes we're talking about things that people haven't talked about that have been bothering people for a long time. It's very delicate. There are a lot of feelings about it. Underneath the diversity topic is a lot of anger and hostility and fear. We've got to know that. We've got to be prepared for that.

Several participants acknowledged the burden on them as pioneering change agents and the wear and tear they were experiencing. One participant remarked, "This is a high burnout area. Aspirins don't take care of the headache."

Most of the participants, and many others in this field, periodically get discouraged. They regularly disagree with colleagues, clients, and friends. They get the sense that for every three steps forward there are at least two steps backward. Yet they stay. They persist because they see the promise in this amorphous thing called diversity.

Are Racism and Sexism the Central Issues?

A fundamental question is what aspects of diversity should we focus on trying to achieve in the workplace. The following was excerpted from an exchange among Walt Tornow, vice president of research and publication at the Center; Bernardo Ferdman; and Elsie Cross.

Tornow [to Elsie Cross]: My understanding of your definition of diversity is that it aims for the elimination or amelioration of "isms"—getting rid of oppression. How would you feel about another kind of definition, which I think is a little bit along the lines of Bernardo's multiculturalism approach, that encourages diversity of all kinds and not just demographic diversity—that is, diversity of sex or ethnicity? Shouldn't we encourage diversity or heterogeneity in such things as perspectives, styles, and thinking, so that we can be as adaptive as possible in the current environment of uncertainty and change?

Ferdman: I see those two things as going together. Talking about race and gender, you start realizing the way people have oppressed people based on group memberships, but group memberships are real. There's a richness that comes out of group memberships. That's the other side of it. How do we understand, how do we create some richness, some benefits, some kind of positive perspective on differences? Racism and sexism see differences as negative. We don't always have a clear vision of what the other side of it is. That's where cultural differences come in.

I do see them as tied to groups. When people start going back to their idea that each person is unique, each is different, we can't forget that that differentness doesn't occur in isolation; it is strongly influenced by group connections. If we forget the group connections, then we're just saying we're all unique individuals but without any context. That's been the philosophy all along, and that's been used as a way to keep people down.

Elsie Cross: I think this work is political. What I have tried to do is to bring my political analysis of this society and of these issues into some way of doing social change in organizations. The oppressor is the problem. In the United States, starting with slavery, it was the oppressor who said there were some people in this country who were less than others. And we still suffer from that notion today. Women are subordinate to men, and all people of color are subordinate to white people. If you can get around that, I'd like to come join you. I don't think there is a way around it.

These different ways of defining or framing the issue of diversity highlight the controversy about whether racism and sexism are central. Some participants argue for a broad definition that encompasses many types of differences, whereas others argue that diversity work must concentrate on differences of race and sex. Nearly 56% of the conference participants agreed with the prework statement that "Racism and sexism have to be the primary targets in any diversity initiative," suggesting this is an important issue for a number of people.

As noted earlier, this controversy is partly a function of the newness of the field. It is still evolving, and we need to keep this in mind as we debate the issues. According to Price Cobbs, the field is now in its third generation. The first generation was an extension of the civil rights movement in the 1960s. The second came about as women became part of the affected classes in the mid to late 1970s. The third started in the early to mid 1980s when we began to recognize the demographics shaping our economy. As the field evolves, the definition of diversity is becoming more inclusive. A demographic focus, however, still dominates.

The controversy is partly semantic. Most participants believe that diversity should not be seen strictly in terms of sex and race, even though some view these as the heart of the matter. Elsie Cross commented, for example, "Ameliorating racism and sexism is a means to an end—seeing people as equals." Cobbs noted that the ultimate goal of diversity is to individualize, but we must first explore the issue of whiteness. He pointed out that Colin Powell, former chief of staff of the U.S. Army, won't equate gays in the military with blacks in the military. For many, he explained, the core issues revolve around race. "If we can get through, truly get through, some of the racial issues, then some of the other issues will become clearer."

Other participants leaned toward an inclusive definition of diversity. Kay Iwata, a diversity consultant who has conducted assessments and run diversity leadership development and education programs for many corporations, for example, was asked whether she agreed that if diversity initiatives don't include all folks, they are not going to work. Iwata responded that an organization's culture has to be factored into where to begin this work, but she added, "I see diversity as inclusive, collective, not 'What's in it for me.'" Iwata and others seem to feel that such inclusiveness will prevent some people, white men and others, from feeling alienated, resentful, and resistant to the changes called for in many diversity initiatives.

Bob Davis, from the American Institute for Managing Diversity, also believes that everyone must be involved. "You have to understand the impact of the organization and its culture on everyone in the organization," he said in a session that he led. Differences on any dimension are considered in his approach. He even used a latecomer to the session as an example of diversity. The latecomer is at a disadvantage because of that difference. The diversity challenge, as with any difference, is to reduce tension, to remake the group to put that person on an equal basis with the insiders—in this case those who came on time.

Backlash from white men was found to be the most serious weakness in the diversity efforts of organizations in *The New Leaders* (Morrison, 1992), and it was a topic of concern during the conference. Another concern that may be somewhat allayed by defining diversity broadly is the fragmentation, or infighting, that often takes place among nontraditional groups themselves. Gloria Bonilla-Santiago identified infighting as an important issue during a panel discussion. She noted the lack of understanding among ethnic groups and the struggles among them for power and resources:

> How do we deal with blacks who have come into positions of power who will do the same thing to Latinos and Asians and Latinos who will do the same thing? How do we move forward in an equitable way? If blacks move forward only, or Latinos move forward, or women move forward without the other groups, then we're in trouble.

Elsie Cross noted that "white men get the rap for all the oppression" but that many white women are racist, many men of color are sexist, and many women of color oppress members of other ethnic groups. Price Cobbs also noted that we are now coming to the realization that blacks and other nontraditionals have issues with one another, not just with whites, and that this is a sensitive "eggshell" issue. He claimed that an issue of the 1990s is that we are all retreating into our own tribes, looking for identity around a single dimension. There are support groups springing up not only for women and members of ethnic groups but also for gays and lesbians, Christians, people over forty, and so on. The problem comes when they don't support one another, and that, Cobbs warned, is happening more frequently in the workplace.

Some participants at the conference were bothered by the visible patterns of segregation they see in organizations, where employee groups are demographically homogeneous; for instance where black managers lunch only with other blacks. Susan Jackson, a professor and consultant on strategic human-resource management and diversity issues, commented, "It disturbs me that people who are advocating diversity are segregating themselves." Elsie Cross pointed out, however, that we need to flip the coin to understand this behavior, and ask, "Why do white people lunch together?" Do we assume, she challenged, that the blacks ought to join the whites because the whites have more value? Derald Sue, a psychology professor and consultant who specializes in multicultural issues, also addressed the issue of ethnic groups "clustering." "People cluster for validation," he explained, but it bothers some of his white students. Sue defines clustering as the forming of groups by people with similar characteristics. "Why is it so difficult for you to go to them," he asks these students, "if you think integration is so important?"

Despite the explanations and suggestions offered, the idea of segregation, even during lunch hour, is offensive to some. Being more inclusive rather than focusing solely on visible group diversity has a great deal of appeal to many participants. The challenge, however, appears to involve culture and context as well as philosophical ideals. The definitions of diversity used in organizations may reflect all of these factors and help explain why there is so much variation from one organization to another. The goal for diversity at the City of San Diego, for example, makes no mention of race, sex, or any other specific difference. The goal, according to Danelle Scarborough, the project leader for the city's diversity commitment program, is:

An environment where differences are valued and all employees are a productive part of a high-performing team delivering services to our community.

Dawn Cross, corporate director for diversity at Corning, explained that certain differences are highlighted in her company's definition of diversity:

An organizational-change process designed to eliminate barriers based on race, gender, and ethnicity, and to create a work environment where every employee is able to achieve his or her potential.

Even though the definitions and goals may differ, both Dawn Cross and Scarborough agree that race and sex differences are at the core of their diversity effort, but that the effort is meant to be inclusive. "If we can make a dent on race, gender, and ethnicity," Dawn Cross remarked, "we can cover anything." Although there are a broad range of opinions about the scope of this work, this is the prevailing view of diversity. It may be a temporary definition, for the field and organizations are still evolving, but it is for many a workable compromise that recognizes a few key visible, permanent differences that we have been grappling with for many years.

Why Is Developing Diversity so Difficult?

Discrimination is prohibited by law. Educational programs about the value of diversity have been taking place for years. Policies supporting diversity are popping up in organizations across the country. Why aren't we seeing more progress? What makes this issue such a difficult one to deal with in organizations?

Before the conference, 82% of conference participants agreed with the statement from the prework that "Prejudice is still the biggest advancement barrier for nontraditional managers." These opinions match the research findings documented in *The New Leaders*. Of the 21 barriers to diversity identified through interviews with managers from sixteen corporations, prejudice is at the top of the list. In that book, prejudice is defined as equating a difference with a deficiency (pp. 34-35). People who look different or have a different background, for example, are often viewed as being less qualified or less able. Negative stereotypes about blacks, women, and members of other groups shape that perception. Prejudice, in its many subtle forms, continues to pervade decisions made in organizations, even in the 1990s.

Ann Morrison noted in her talk on "The New Leaders" that most people are perplexed about how to eliminate or prevent prejudice, and many managers are convinced that prejudice cannot be combatted in their lifetime. For one thing, prejudice is embedded in our society. Elsie Cross pointed out that a fundamental value assumption in the United States is that African-Americans and other people of color are inferior to whites. She also noted that originally even the U.S. Constitution did not encompass blacks, or women, or even poor white people who didn't hold property. We may have achieved desegration in this country, she said, citing Andrew Hacker's recent book *Two Nations* (1991), but society has resegregated in terms of housing, education, etc. The influence of society's norms and practices is difficult for any organization to counteract.

Price Cobbs spoke about the dissertations and other research he has seen on prejudice. One factor that he believes makes prejudice so difficult to address as individuals is that "most of us consciously and ethically think we are fair." That is, most people aren't overt bigots but they also don't acknowledge their prejudices. In our culture, he said, contact with difference is hardly benign:

> I remember a Schick ad where the voice-over for the guy shaving was, "Sometimes to be different is to be better." They could only make that ad, and people would only understand it, if the assumption were the opposite: To be different is to be less than.

Prejudice may weave into other significant barriers that keep many nontraditional managers from advancing and contributing at their full capacity in organizations. In "The New Leaders" presentation, it was noted that five other important barriers were found in the research documented in *The New Leaders*: (1) career planning and development which has failed to give many nontraditional employees the breadth of experience and credentials required to compete for senior management posts; (2) a lonely, unsupportive, and even hostile working environment for many nontraditional managers, particularly in upper management; (3) lack of "corporate savvy" or political skills on the part of nontraditional managers, which makes them feel vulnerable and seem awkward; (4) the fact that people are generally more comfortable dealing with people of their own kind; and (5) difficulty balancing career and family demands, especially for women.

Addressing each of these barriers is challenging in itself, but the fact that there are so many barriers, even in the most progressive organizations in this country, adds to the degree of difficulty. Dawn Cross responded to a question, in her session on "Corning's Diversity Initiative," about the problems still facing the company concerning diversity. Even at Corning, a company that is regularly praised and admired for its advancements in diversity, problems still persist. She mentioned that the chairman's direct reports are still all white men, and the executive group is only beginning to become integrated. The lack of role models is, therefore, a problem. She also noted that people continue to operate with old assumptions and stereotypes. The use of some of the new policies is still low, and there continues to be a lack of comfort and awkwardness working with people who are different. Many nontraditionals, she said, still don't feel included as members of the team.

Derald Sue and Elsie Cross also addressed the kinds of barriers that make developing diversity so difficult in many organizations. Along with negative stereotypes and continuing discrimination in the workplace, Sue referred to communication-style differences among different groups, and the culture-bound values of organizations.

Earlier in the day, in a session on the competencies needed for managing diversity, Sue had told this story. A math teacher in this country gave a white student and a Nigerian exchange student the following problem: "There are four birds in a tree. You shoot one. How many are left?" This would seem to many people to be a straightforward question with an obvious answer: three. But, as Sue pointed out, answers can vary. The U.S. student answered "three," but the Nigerian student answered "none." When asked about his answer, the latter explained that the other birds would fly away when they heard the shot.

Like students, employees are also likely to have a variety of perspectives on the world. Sue also told the story of Filipino nurses in a hospital who weren't performing well. It was finally discovered that these nurses found it very difficult to admit that they did not understand what their supervisors were telling them to do and, as a result, were not getting adequate instruction. In their culture, to admit you do not understand implies that the teacher is deficient. The solution, Sue said, was for the supervisors to demonstrate what needed to be done and then to ask each nurse to demonstrate. Corrections could be made if something was done wrong.

Adjusting to people who may see things differently is often not a difficult process. But all too often, it happens that the Nigerian student is written off as weird and the Filipino nurses are dismissed for being incompetent. Their perspectives are not recognized or appreciated. And, many argue, because they have dark skin or are female, their views are all too easy to discount.

Dawn Cross, in her session, also emphasized that, at the systemic level, standards are embedded in the organization's culture, policies, and procedures.

Because the images of success in many organizations are based on traits normed on white men, she said, even the best-intentioned people try to get people of color and white women to fit into the old image rather than creating new images for success.

Elsie Cross mentioned other problems that keep organizations from making headway in developing diversity: trying to fix the victim rather than the oppressors; victims sometimes colluding with their oppressors (for survival or because they want to be liked and accepted)—for instance, by not pointing out racism or sexism; assuming that winners don't make mistakes (rather than encouraging experimentation and innovation, managers shun risk-taking and shy away from others who do); assuming that excellent performers develop themselves; assuming that corporate America is a meritocracy ("It's not merit," she explained, "it's how I feel about you that gets you the promotion"); and white people not knowing how to give feedback to nontraditionals, and wanting to avoid conflict.

Another problem that gets in the way of progress on developing diversity (and other initiatives) is what Bob Davis calls *root guards*. Every organization has them, he said. These are the people who say, "Why change? We're successful as we are." They defend the organization's roots, or the basic tenets of culture, even though they may be dysfunctional. Davis described several common dysfunctional roots, such as the family root in which "father knows best" and runs the firm, lifetime employment is standard, and outsiders (inlaws or stepchildren as analogies) can never become real family members.

Overcoming these roots and other problems takes a special effort. Organizations that have begun to act on diversity often have to spurn tradition and inertia. In his experience, three reasons most often provoke them to action. The most common reason is pain on the bottom line, internal or external. A diverse work force and poor people managers, for example, could stimulate action, or changing requirements for products and services because of increasing customer diversity. Another thing that incites organizations to action, Davis said, is a CEO who has gotten the message about diversity. Employee groups also kindle action by putting upward pressure on executives; "We can make more of a contribution," these groups argue, "if changes are made."

To begin the change process, however, "the gain has to exceed the pain," according to Davis. When an organization is not experiencing a crisis, the challenge is to convince executives, including the root guards, that there is pain in the future. That represents another barrier in many organizations, because getting people to feel future pain when business seems to be going along just fine is a very difficult proposition.

It is obvious that there are a variety of problems and barriers that make diversity an intimidating goal in organizations. These difficulties are often reflected in the tools and techniques used in existing diversity initiatives, as we will see later. One final barrier we will mention here is that the road to success in developing diversity is still largely an unblazed trail. There is a lot of ambiguity which makes many people nervous. Susan Jackson said, "Corporate America is just venturing out on a new journey for which there is no template of success to date." It is a venture that requires strong leadership, for the potential gains are attractive to many.

What Are the Potential Outcomes of Developing Diversity?

Despite the sometimes seemingly insurmountable difficulties in developing diversity, nearly all the participants agreed before and after the conference with the statement, "Diversity should remain a top priority for organizations regardless of economic conditions or other business hardships." Perhaps some felt diversity should remain a priority precisely because it is such a challenge. Many agreed because they see enormous potential gains for their organization.

At Corning, diversity is so important that it is one of the corporation's three objectives, along with quality and performance. Dawn Cross explained that the model used at Corning to facilitate discussion of these objectives incorporates what is expected to happen as a result of the involvement in diversity, including higher retention, greater utilization of employees and improved performance, respect for differences, enhanced team effectiveness, and higher morale. At the individual level, expectations include increased commitment, greater career satisfaction, and a high level of performance. A climate survey is used to track some of these factors.

Although numerical representation is often used to demonstrate the benefits of a diversity initiative, some executives and consultants take a broader perspective. Elsie Cross, for example, outlined some of the characteristics of a successfully diverse organization: Employees are able to deal with conflict; employees respect people; the organization empowers people; the climate is humanistic; employees can talk openly, including about issues of race and sex; people with different styles manage effectively; and employees are evaluated and promoted based on their performance, not their role.

Dana Friedman, of the Families and Work Institute, also has a broad perspective on diversity, particularly concerning the benefits of work-life programs. She commented: "True family friendliness is not the number of programs you have, or even the quality of these programs; it's what happens as the people use them." For example, if you've got people working part-time and you believe that you can never promote them, that's the problem. This can be seen in law firms in which the partners refuse to count part-time work toward partnership. If it takes eight years of full-time work to make partner, and some lawyers want to work half-time, why shouldn't it be fine to require sixteen years for them to make partner? Changing that mindset is the ultimate benefit, for the lawyers themselves and the company as a whole.

Employees give more of themselves and increase their productivity when diversity has become embedded in the organization's culture, Friedman noted. She and others referred to the increased trust factor that can result from a diversity effort, which can contribute to productivity. Susan Jackson noted that employees' positive perceptions of organizational climate contribute to high-performing work teams. Employees' views of their job security, cooperation, the quality of employee relationships, and communications were all tied to team performance. Because diversity should affect employees' perceptions of the work climate, it should also affect their productivity in teams.

The potential benefits of diversity are even broader. Gene Andrews, manager, workforce diversity, at General Electric, for example, was asked about GE's commitment to diversity "beyond just the organization." "Could you speak a little bit about the broader social responsibility in terms of what you're doing?" a participant queried. Andrews said that GE is proud to devote some $40 million toward major education initiatives. Half of that sum is aimed at doubling the number of disadvantaged students finishing high school and going on to college, particularly in GE's plant locations. He said the results have been remarkable. In four years, he said they have more than doubled the number of disadvantaged students in college. Another goal is to increase the number of faculty of color in colleges and universities. GE also adopts schools. These diversity programs benefit the community as well as GE.

Clearly, many benefits associated with diversity are vague, indirect, and long term. It is important, however, to measure and monitor these outcomes, whether they involve changes in attitudes, knowledge, behavior, or other results. Allen Kraut, a professor of management and a management consultant, who retired as IBM's head of personnel research, warned that we send the wrong message if we simply assume that benefits will accrue and exempt diversity efforts from evaluation. People question whether it is really important. Also, tracking the benefits helps clarify the purposes and goals of diversity activities, whether they have to do with building the organization's competitive edge or social change.

Kraut warned, however, that practitioners can be sidetracked in monitoring benefits. Be careful about who you are trying to convince, he cautioned, particularly given the influence of the press and the popular lists of "best companies."

> If we get our name in print, and they say we're one of ten or twenty best companies, we are likely to believe it. I hate to be cynical, but I think sometimes we behave in a way that suggests if others write about us, we think we've really got it down pat. Others write about us and tell us we're great, so we think our employees think the same thing. That may or may not be true.

Although improving the organization's public image is a worthy goal, it cannot substitute for other benefits.

The potential benefits and outcomes of developing diversity are also discussed below in the chapter "How Can Organizational Commitment to Diversity Be Developed?" (where we cover the payoffs that get the attention of top management) and in the chapter "How Should a Diversity Initiative Proceed?" (where we look at the techniques for building more accountability for diversity into organizations). Statistical diversity goals are described in more detail in the latter as well.

Although we have not spent much time on statistical goals and benefits in this section, that does not mean these don't represent a critical part of any diversity initiative. Diversity activities can and should significantly affect an organization's personnel profiles. Xerox Corporation is a good example of the changes that are possible. Between 1964 and 1990, Xerox increased the representation of women at the officer and manager levels from a mere 1% to 22%, according to Ted Payne, manager of corporate employment and college relations. The representation of people of color at the officer and manager level grew from only 1% to 19%. And nearly 25% of Xerox's vice presidents and directors in 1991 were nontraditional managers.

"Xerox started off looking like every other company. The data prove it can be done," Payne remarked. Few will argue that this kind of change takes enormous effort, or that progress is slow and fragile, but many practitioners believe such change is beneficial and even necessary. For that reason, they persist in pioneering in this area. They pursue commitment from the top, and they proceed to take action to develop diversity. In the remainder of this book we will discuss how people do this work.

Chapter 2
HOW CAN ORGANIZATIONAL COMMITMENT TO DIVERSITY BE DEVELOPED?

We had asked Dawn Cross, corporate director of diversity at Corning, to discuss the range of her company's activities. Corning is known for having a comprehensive diversity initiative that includes such things as gender workshops, racial-awareness workshops, third-party counseling, alternative work schedules, programs for addressing work/family issues, career-planning systems, and the legitimization and encouragement of coaching relationships. In addition, the initiative is strongly tied to the push for quality, with a Women's Quality Improvement Team dedicated to helping the company become free of gender constraints, and a Black Progress Quality Improvement Team intended to assist it in identifying and removing barriers that prevent Corning from fully utilizing each black employee's contributions in meeting corporate goals. As Cross began explaining the history and rationale of diversity at Corning, one of the first questions from participants had to do with why it had gotten involved in diversity. In particular, why was Corning committed to diversity? According to Dawn Cross, one of the key reasons was that in 1987, top management noticed that African-American women and men and white women had exceptionally high attrition rates—in the neighborhood of 15 to 16%. It was estimated that the cost of hiring and training each person was $40,000, with the departure of 50 people bringing the costs into the range of $2 million, excluding fees to headhunters for finding replacements. Cross said Corning got involved in diversity in part because of this cost of doing business. Such costs were counter to the emphasis on quality, which was becoming a strong component of its culture.

The attrition costs weren't the only reason Corning got involved. Other factors entered into the equation as well. In particular, the high attrition rate goes against its corporate value to respect the individual. Corning puts a premium on treating employees well and the high attrition rate indicated it wasn't doing as good a job of that as it would have liked. Furthermore, the high attrition rate showed that although the company was good at recruiting white women and African-American women and men, it wasn't as good at optimizing the careers of this population. And finally it was running into difficulty with the expectations of new recruits throughout the organization who anticipated a family-friendly and diverse company.

In a session on Xerox Corporation's experiences with diversity interventions, led by Ted Payne, a similar question was asked. Like Dawn Cross, Payne spoke of galvanizing events which pushed Xerox's commitment towards diversity. He discussed the riots in 1963 and 1968 in Rochester, the city where Xerox then had its corporate headquarters; this led Xerox to ask what it could do to contribute to better race relations there. It made a commitment to diversity as a way of dealing with the changes in the Rochester community wrought by the riots and as a way of protecting their investment in factories and plants in the event of future riots.

Danelle Scarborough, in her session on "San Diego's Commitment to Diversity," also shared an organization's rationale to commit to diversity. Scarborough described a city government of 10,000 employees demoralized because of budget cuts and other painful externally driven issues. They were looking for a way to make the work force feel valued and productive during downsizing. They wanted to make the work force, of which 37% were people of color, feel engaged, important, and valued during this period of change, and saw an emphasis on diversity as a way to accomplish this.

Throughout the conference, questions about organizational investment in and commitment to diversity came up frequently. Although we had only planned to have two sessions emphasizing commitment, several of the sessions ended up focusing on the topic. In addition, many of the ad hoc sessions, which were requested by participants, emphasized commitment as well. During the conference researchers such as Susan Jackson provided research-based rationales for diversity; consultants such as Price Cobbs, Elsie Cross, Kay Iwata, Ginger Lapid-Bogda, and Terri Sligh shared approaches for developing organizational commitment; and diversity directors internal to corporations shared their experiences. In postconference activities, the theme remained central to participants as well. In the postconference poll, we asked those participants who were responsible for implementing diversity initiatives if they had taken any action based on the conference. About a quarter reported that they had been actively engaged in trying to garner commitment from the organization for a diversity intervention. These efforts focused on three areas: (1) communicating to the organization why it is important to invest in diversity; (2) gaining the commitment of top management; and (3) getting commitment from the rest of the organization. These three themes reflect the basic issues about commitment discussed at the conference.

Why Invest in Diversity?

During the conference several reasons were offered for why organizations do and should invest in diversity. They ranged from the strategic to moral responsibilities. Many people recommended using a combination of both types of reasons to encourage commitment.

Strategic Reasons. Several people argued for the importance of strategic concerns in making the case for diversity. In the fictional scenario that formed the basis of a panel discussion, Frederick A. Miller, a consultant who specializes in helping corporations conceptualize and launch diversity efforts, argued that diversity must be central to the organization. He said one way to do that is to make a business case for diversity; he warned that ignoring the business case can lead to its becoming a peripheral issue.

Susan Jackson elaborated on the theme of relying on diversity to meet business needs. She led a session about the importance of customizing diversity issues in terms of implications of the business strategy for the organization. Her perspective has been shaped by her own research and by her observations of several diversity efforts in large corporations (for case examples, see Jackson & Associates, 1992). She contended that diversity efforts are critical because they can address strategic imperatives such as cost, innovation, quality, customer service, speed, and globalization. In her talk, Jackson put the greatest emphasis on the first four imperatives, stressing that organizations should consider their company's strategic imperatives and customize their diversity initiatives to fit their own unique situation.

Cost. Like Dawn Cross, Jackson feels that the increased turnover associated with poorly managed diversity can be tied to cost. Her research looked at the top-management teams of 93 large bank holding companies (Jackson, Brett, Sessa, Cooper, Julin, & Peyronnin, 1991). Although she didn't find diversity in terms of race and gender, she did find it in age, tenure, education, college curriculum, military experience, and non-industry experience. Her study found that there was more rapid turnover among members of more diverse teams. It was found that dissimilarity doesn't necessarily cause people to leave; rather, it's being in a heterogeneous group that seems to create turnover. According to Jackson, "It was as if everyone was somewhat less comfortable in these groups and turned over more quickly." She pointed out that a consultant might say to this group, all of whom were white males, "You need to learn how to manage diversity, you are not comfortable with it. . . . You really should have a diversity intervention here." The more heterogeneous groups in terms of age, tenure, education, and experience had more turnover. Jackson believes this is because the diversity is not well managed.

Jackson further links turnover to cost by citing a 1991 study by Ulrich, Halbrook, Meder, Struchlik, and Thorpe that ties the average tenure of employees in different teams to the performance of the team in terms of return on assets. The study found that the teams with greater average tenure were more effective financially; the implication of this is that greater team tenure leads to some types of effectiveness. This evidence suggests that attempts to reduce attrition in diverse teams can be associated with reduced costs.

Innovation. According to Jackson, another link between diversity and strategy involves the relation between diversity and innovative problem solving. Several studies have shown that groups composed of diverse people have more creative problem-solving abilities. A weakness inherent in most of this research is that it is conducted with college students who often work on trivial tasks. Often these results are not convincing to the business community with its focus on significant problems faced by mature adults.

To respond to this issue, Jackson and her colleague, Karen Bantel, conducted a study of top-management teams in the banking industry (Bantel & Jackson, 1989). They used the composition of top-management teams to predict which banks would be most innovative. Banking experts determined the degree to which a business action was considered innovative. They found strong evidence that diversity in terms of career and functional background of team members was significantly associated with innovation. In other words, the greater the diversity among team members, the more innovative the bank.

To further the argument for the relationship of diversity to innovation, Jackson refers to the difficulty of getting people who have different occupational specializations and job experiences to communicate and innovate. She cites Rosabeth Kanter's 1989 work on innovative organizations which concluded that the most innovative organizations focus on pooling, linking, and aligning across organization boundaries. In other words, they have well-developed strategies for cross-functional communication. It is fairly obvious that organizations which can promote cross-group communication are likely to be more innovative.

Quality. The link between diversity and quality is made through the notion of teamwork. Teamwork is an extremely important idea to the quality movement. Everyone has to be included to make the product, service, or business better. According to Jackson, research by David Ulrich and his colleagues (1991) points out that the quality of production in twelve plants is linked to organizational climate. Specifically, aspects of organizational climate reflected in indices of cooperation, the quality of employee relationships, and communication are linked to production. In her opinion, diversity-intervention efforts can have an impact on these. Diversity interventions intend to improve relationships and channels of communication. She points out that companies like Xerox which are pursuing both total-quality and diversity initiatives are in a unique position to deal with relationship and communication issues. Both types of initiatives deal with the contributions of teams to effective operations.

Customer service. Quality is linked to a fit between service delivery and the person receiving the service. Service has to do with the human exchange, to some extent the matching of characteristics of the customers and the service personnel. To demonstrate the point that customers are more satisfied with a service if there is some match between people delivering the service and the people receiving it, Jackson cited a study by J. Lehtinen (1991) that examines how different cultures perceive service. This study points out that different culture groups expect different types of service; for example, in some cultures people prefer familiarity (as opposed to formality) during an exchange. This suggests that in customer service it is important to be in contact with key customer constituencies. And this translates into developing skills for emphasizing managing relationships with different types of people. In order to improve customer service, it is important to have people who understand the needs of different customer groups.

Although there was a lot of emphasis on linking diversity interventions to strategic concerns as a rationale for investing in diversity at the conference, it was by no means the only rationale discussed. Many people also took a strong stance that morality and values should be used as an organizational rationale for diversity.

Moral Reasons. There are those who see the lack of sex and racial diversity in an organization as a moral and political problem. Elsie Cross, for instance, tends to focus on the moral reasons for diversity, pointing out how the social tensions in our society play out in corporate settings. According to Cross, business problems are caused by oppression of certain groups by others.

When she starts an intervention at a company she stresses to the CEO and other top executives that the intervention will concentrate on ameliorating oppression. She wants the top of the organization to take responsibility for the intervention on moral grounds because it is the right thing to do.

Several of the participants have suggested using both the strategic and the moral approach and developing a rationale where these approaches can coexist. In fact, the rationales offered by the representatives of Corning, Xerox, and the City of San Diego, which emphasized issues such as attrition, riots, and a demoralized work force, reflect a blend of both. Kay Iwata suggested during the conference that there isn't one best way to make the argument for diversity. She says to go with the source of the push in the organization; if it is values, then use that as a rationale; if it is business, go with the business case.

Gaining Commitment of Top Management

Although the rationale for diversity development interventions was an area for debate at the conference, the critical need to get top-management commitment for a diversity intervention was not. The preconference poll asked participants to rank the effectiveness of a set of corporate diversity practices. Eighty percent of conference attendees ranked "Active intervention by top management in a diversity initiative" as the most effective diversity practice.

Several sessions throughout the conference featured stories about top managers who made a difference to the success of a diversity effort through their personal actions and activities. For example, Gene Andrews said that the primary force behind diversity at GE has been chairman Jack Welch. Andrews tells the story of Welch meeting for a full day with a group of white women and people of color at the GE management development center to get information about the obstacles they faced and their concerns. He told the company's top executives that one of the five key issues for GE to address in the 1990s is diversity. Andrews cited several other occasions where Welch acted as a champion for diversity and said that he has put some punch into his advocacy by holding managers responsible for focusing on diversity. In a 1991 meeting with the 120 company officers, Welch told them to be prepared in 1992 to discuss what they had done to advance diversity in their operations.

Like Gene Andrews, Dawn Cross of Corning pointed to the impact of chairman involvement in diversity. When asked about her greatest learnings about the journey towards diversity, she said:

> Top management commitment is one that comes through loud and clear for me. Our chairman has been instrumental in (a) raising the issue and (b) driving it through. That has been absolutely essential to our success.

Had it not been for the chairman's commitment, which has been consistent and persistent, we would not be where we are today.

Ted Payne of Xerox also strongly advocated the power of top-management commitment. He thinks CEO involvement is critical because the organization that is trying to grow more diverse is surrounded by institutions and communities that are going in the opposite direction. As an example of CEO commitment, he cited how David Kearns, when he was the CEO of Xerox, handled downsizing. When Xerox decided to reduce the number of personnel, the question of criteria came up. Should it be last in and first out, a policy which would jeopardize affirmative-action goals? Or should it be some other method? The legal department was on one side of the issue and the affirmative-action staff on the other. The legal department said, "We need to be defensive and make sure that we protect ourselves from lawsuits." Affirmative action said, "If you take last in, first out, you're going to undo all the progress we've made with women and minorities in the business." The person sitting in the middle was David Kearns. He listened and, according to Payne, made the decision that Xerox would maintain the representation of women and minorities in the business even if he had to go to court and defend it. He also published a letter that went to every employee that announced that Xerox would remain committed to affirmative action and drive itself to its goals. Payne said that Kearns wanted to be sure that nobody had any questions about that.

Why CEO Support Is Essential. In addition to the testimonial support for the involvement of top management, people provided conceptual views as to why support from the top is essential. Bob Davis stressed that diversity is about empowering everyone to do their best and CEO involvement is essential for this to happen. Davis believes that they must be committed to making diversity a core value so that diversity considerations will be taken into account when tough choices emerge.

Ginger Lapid-Bogda led a session on gaining top-management commitment, based on her article, "How to Win Senior Management's Support for Diversity" (1992). She outlined seven reasons why senior-management support is essential.

(1) Top management sets organizational priorities. Unless diversity is an organizational priority, it won't happen. Lapid-Bogda cites Gene Andrews' example of how Jack Welch of GE made diversity an organizational priority.

(2) The senior team has symbolic impact, so it is important that they be on board early. Employees going through diversity-related training should ask

trainers if they have worked with top management and if they are committed. For an intervention to be successful it is important to have answers. Through their own participation in the process, senior managers can affect the progress of others.

(3) Senior managers can link diversity to business initiatives. It is the job of the senior team to decide the strategy and business reasons for diversity interventions. The consultant or trainer shouldn't be making these linkages alone.

(4) Senior teams allocate organizational resources. Diversity efforts require money and it is essential to have top-management support for these expenditures.

(5) It is critical to include diversity in any organizational vision. Otherwise, it is difficult to get a diversity change effort going and only the senior team can put their stamp of approval on diversity as part of the fundamental vision.

(6) Dealing with organizational resistance is inevitable in a diversity intervention. Senior-team members need to be in a position where they don't collude with the resisters and they need to say to them, "I understand that this is upsetting or you're concerned about this; let's talk about what your concerns are and we'll figure out a way to get you on board with this."

(7) The senior team needs to work in this area even though they may say they don't. Lapid-Bogda points out that most senior-management teams really do need to do practical work in this arena.

Functions of Top Management. Another way to understand the value of top-management commitment was to look at the role and function of top managers. Kay Iwata and Terri Sligh, a specialist in human resource and organization development, led a discussion on the roles of top management. They asked small groups of participants to specify the behaviors of a committed CEO. The question they asked was, "From a leadership perspective, what does the leadership commitment look like?" They received the following answers.

(1) Top management should honestly communicate the value of diversity to employees in terms of the organization vision. Communication helps establish a culture supportive of diversity. At U S West, Inc., one tool under development to facilitate honest communication is a set of diversity questions to be added to the quarterly climate survey. That information will be shared across the organization as well as with the board and will be used to facilitate discussion of the issues. Other companies represented at the conference used opinion polls as well. Another form of communication, used at Procter &

Gamble Co., is the memorandum, which in one case was used to explain that junior-level people were added to a key operating committee meeting in order to increase the diversity of contributors. Other places for communicating diversity values include recruiting brochures, company newsletters, annual reports, and informational videos.

(2) Top management needs to be constant in purpose so the company stands committed in the face of resistance and backlash. Kay Iwata suggested one way this can be accomplished is through tying diversity to other key initiatives—such as quality—which the organization is already committed to. She called this process of integrating various organizational goals a "strategic weave," and suggested interventions that support multiple agendas.

(3) Top management should function as role models. This includes selecting a diverse group of direct reports like Jack Welch of GE has done with appointments of African-Americans and white women as presidents of line organizations. This also includes acting appropriately and comfortably as a member of a diverse group and thereby setting expectations for others. Additionally, participation in diversity training-and-development activities is a way of demonstrating and modeling the importance of a diversity intervention.

(4) The managers at the top of an organization should use the performance appraisal and pay systems to introduce messages about accountability for diversity. This includes both holding others accountable for unacceptable behavior with respect to diversity and rewarding achievements in the area. Richard McCormick of U S West was cited as an example of a CEO who requires senior-team members to report on their individual activities in support of diversity.

(5) Senior management needs to understand the barriers people of color and white women face and set policies against exclusion. Senior managers need to address these barriers just as they would technical and financial problems.

(6) Top managers need to make tough choices about diversity compared to other company values. The CEO must understand and be willing to make decisions that encourage diversity. Core values such as diversity need to be lived and consistently demonstrated.

(7) Senior managers should be willing to change the infrastructure and systems in accordance with diversity interventions and to provide resources for such changes. Top managers have to be willing to change long-standing systems in order to institutionalize diversity as a core value.

Approaches to Convincing Top Management to Invest in Diversity.
The focus during the conference on the importance of top-management com-

mitment and the role of senior managers led several participants to ask how to persuade reluctant CEOs to support efforts to promote greater work-force diversity.

One type of question posed was essentially, "Can you change a CEO's values with regard to diversity?" In response to a question of this nature, Susan Jackson remarked that although she feels top-management support is important, she is not convinced that it is the best use of resources to devote many hours to trying to change reluctant senior management, who may be leaving the organization soon anyway. Jackson feels that it is more important to get top management on board in terms of resources and symbolic activities. However, because the time horizon for making meaningful change is so long, her advice is to focus on the leaders the next level down who represent the wave of the future.

In response to a question about how to change a CEO's values, the participants in Kay Iwata's and Terri Sligh's session on leadership commitment had some suggestions.

One strategy is to use some significant emotional event to get top management involved. One participant suggested having some type of training that deals deeply with emotions, with the goal of having the event open the CEO's eyes to diversity.

A second strategy is to get an ally close to the CEO to work on getting the CEO on board. One participant said she found out that one of the more influential top executives had five daughters. She found him personally interested in diversity because of his family situation and asked him to ask his oldest daughter what she was experiencing in business and how she felt about it. He did that and they had conversations about it. He went to the CEO and helped him realize the significance of diversity issues and was successful in persuading him to commit to them. Eventually this man became the CEO.

A third strategy is to tell people at the officer level what is actually happening in the ranks. Data about this can be collected several ways. Terri Sligh used a focus-group process at Lockheed in which she asked high-potential employees from different demographic groups to identify the major obstacles they faced. Each group then presented the data to the CEO. Sligh tied these presentations about barriers and obstacles to the CEO's core value of treating people equitably. She used his passion for fair treatment as a way to start the journey towards diversity. She was able to get commitment by framing the diversity data in terms of a stated emphasis on equity.

The use of data feedback was mentioned often in response to the general question of how do you get support from top management. Bob Davis was a strong advocate of this practice. He suggested a cultural audit using multiple strategies such as focus groups, interviews, written surveys, and archival searches as a means of collecting data. Feedback of the data helps senior management to see how things are and can convince them to buy into a cultural change.

Allen Kraut said, "Data is extremely powerful in terms of guiding and motivating. It is also a platform for discussing and surfacing issues." He cautioned that data must be collected in a competent way and that management must be a partner in framing and doing the research so that they will feel a sense of ownership about the results.

Ginger Lapid-Bogda also strongly argued for providing top management with data, seeing it as an opportunity to help them better understand the organization. She has developed what she calls a culture audit which focuses on the business issues, what success looks like, and the experience of different groups. It incorporates interviews with top management, employee survey data, data about competitors, and benchmarking data.

Lapid-Bogda suggested keeping the data feedback simple so that it highlights major points. She tries to make it visually stimulating and stressed that it should be provocative. Sanitized data or softened data won't help gain commitment. After presenting the data, she sets it up so the top-management team wrestles with the data, draws conclusions, and links it to real business needs.

She suggested data collection as part of a process for gaining top-management support for diversity. The first step in the process is to get access to top management. She said it is critical to be persistent about dealing with them, and it is necessary to provide them with a convincing rationale as to why they should be involved. She clarifies her expectations of them and then tries to gain access both through the formal structure and through informal channels. She said that patience is very important in this process.

The next step is to build relationships with top management. One way Lapid-Bogda does that is through interviews with each of them, where she tries to get to know them. She also tries to establish credibility and develop an understanding of the business. A key issue is to try to manage the power differentials since both internal and external consultants have less power than top management. She recognizes the differential and accepts it, not taking it too seriously. Personalized conversations with senior management about their lives helps to adjust for the power difference.

Next is to provide senior managers with data as was discussed earlier. Lapid-Bogda works collaboratively with senior managers to link the data to business reasons for diversity. Labor-force demographics, customer demographics, productivity, innovation issues, lawsuits, and complaints are discussed. She helps them focus on what senior management is trying to accomplish with the company.

After that, she tries to identify what other key issues senior managers are facing and how they link those issues to diversity. A further step is to link diversity to other business initiatives such as total quality or self-managing work teams. She works with them to identify the common ground in terms of values, purpose, activities, and so on. She tries to develop ties with programs that are working well and keeps a respectful distance from unhelpful alliances.

The last step is to clarify senior management's role in the intervention. She suggested that as symbolic leaders, they must be visible, committed, and act in congruence with principles of the intervention. As operational leaders, they must define the business issues, authorize the resources, and ask tough questions. And as transformative leaders, they must work cooperatively to create a vision for the organization, change the culture, and work on themselves.

Gaining Commitment From the Organization: Handling Backlash

Although commitment from top management is essential for a diversity intervention, it is also important to get the rest of the organization on board. Middle managers are seen as key players in this; they are likely to be responsible for managing and developing a diverse group. At the conference, there was much discussion on gaining commmitment throughout the organization with most of the discussion focusing on how to handle resistance to diversity interventions. What do you do when there is backlash?

Several of the participants (for instance, Elsie Cross, Ginger Lapid-Bogda, and Price Cobbs) mentioned that resistance is inevitable in a diversity effort. Elsie Cross pointed out that if resistance isn't happening, then change isn't happening. Several different tactics and strategies for dealing with resistance were suggested during the course of the conference.

Elsie Cross argued that resistance needs to be encouraged and welcomed. She likens the concept of backlash to judo to explain her viewpoint. Typically, if you push against something you either fall down or your resistance increases. The mechanics of judo suggest that if you welcome resistance, it comes towards you—the person who is resisting falls into you. So what Elsie Cross tries to do is to ask people who are resisting why they feel that way. It is important to hear their pain. She says as we hear their pain we can ask them what would it be like if you were a white woman in that setting or if you were a black person. She tries to get the person to connect and empathize with others. Elsie's approach is to hear the resisters' pain and to let them know it is important, and through this to get them to try to understand the pain of others.

Ginger Lapid-Bogda had a similar view about the welcoming of resistance. She stressed, however, that top management should play an active role in this process. If top management doesn't try to understand the resistance and try to figure it out, they are colluding with resisters.

Lapid-Bogda also pointed out that, in addition to seriously listening to resisters, top management needs to hold managers accountable for supporting diversity. She told the story of running a training program in an organization in which one guy got up and said to her, "Let's get real here. I believe I own my wife, like I own my house and my car, and if the other men in this group are honest, they will say that they feel the same way." Four other white men in the group agreed with him. At the end of the program, Lapid-Bogda, understanding that this man held extreme views about women and their place in society, asked him, "What is going to get you to come around to being more open to diversity in this organization?" He said, "Senior management's commitment to this. If they hold me accountable, I will do it. If they don't, I will not."

In a session on best-practice companies, Gene Andrews and Dawn Cross both argued that CEO involvement helped in dealing with resistance. Dawn Cross said that the CEO of Corning, James Houghton, has been extremely forceful in getting managers on board.

An additional strategy recommended by the resource people concerned the communication and sharing of data relevant to diversity. According to Gene Andrews, sharing data helps to shatter myths about the progress women and people of color have made within the company. He explained that

> the GE medical systems business starts off its training with a video of the head of the business and its officers. They talk about the myth [of women and minorities getting ahead in large numbers] and then they show the reality by getting out the numbers so that others understand that the representation of women and minorities remains lower than that of white males.

Ted Payne described a similar strategy at Xerox where some resisters held the myth that women and minorities were getting all the good jobs. He explained that they developed a balanced work-force strategy presented in the affirmative-action plans. When data was presented inside the company, they included goals and targets for majority men. This way, white men could see that they were part of the equation. In the past, majority men were there, but only by implication. This new format specifically showed them to be part of the work-force equation. Apparently, it forced division heads and HR heads in one Xerox group to consciously seek to bring in white men at the entry level. People in this group received less satisfactory performance reviews when they failed to meet those goals.

Payne also shared the story of how he and the president of one Xerox division have dealt with backlash. They developed a three-and-a-half page, single-spaced list of people in upper-level positions, and set out to identify the white women and people of color. There was only one—a white woman. Payne carries the list around, and anytime anyone says, "Women and minorities are getting too many promotions," he just pulls this out and says, "Count them."

In Susan Jackson's view, emphasis on the relationship of diversity to strategy is another way of dealing with backlash. Fred Miller agreed. He said that diversity has to be a central part of the organization. Tying it to the business case and to strategic plans helps get middle managers, who are the most vulnerable group to backlash, on board.

Price Cobbs suggested that a key issue with regard to resistance to diversity is understanding whiteness, or what he calls *unearned arrogance.* He suggested that diversity interventions help whites to better understand what it means to be white and how whites are perceived. A first step is for whites to examine how they benefit from being white, to see the benefits they accrue.

Interestingly, many of the whites in his conference sessions had difficulty grasping the concept of whiteness and the privilege it brings. Cobbs, however, pushed them to think about their unequal access to opportunities and their differential treatment. Personal examples from black participants helped to clarify the privileges that whites have. One black participant told a story of being unable to go to a record store without being scrutinized as if he were a thief. Another participant told of the difficulty of finding a Father's Day card with a black father on it.

Whites were then able to get a better understanding of the preferential treatment they receive, both personally and in the organization, and to appreciate the implication of this for others who don't. It also became clear that such self-examination is an arduous task. Cobbs stressed that because of the privileges associated with being white in America, many white men are perceived as arrogant. Understanding this perception and its relationship to privilege is a first step in dealing with diversity and resistance to diversity interventions.

Yet another approach to backlash and to gaining organizational commitment is to focus on the inclusiveness of a diversity intervention. Several people took the tack that a diversity intervention should be an inclusive one that empowers the entire work force. With such an approach, resistance is lessened because resisters are included in the initiative. Bob Davis said that a diversity intervention should create an environment where everyone can contribute to the future. He spoke of transforming an organizational culture into a culture of empowerment in which everyone feels capable of contributing fully to the mission.

Danelle Scarborough also suggested taking an inclusive approach. She stated that in her work as project leader for San Diego's diversity commitment effort, she and her colleagues have sought to create an environment where everyone contributes and differences are valued. Jack McGrory, the City Manager of San Diego, stressed that in order for people to effectively contribute to the team, it is important to create a culture in which they feel comfortable. He said that total organizational commitment is necessary; without it, alienation can occur.

Gene Andrews also stressed that GE views diversity as an inclusive concept. He said:

> Women and minorities alone will not make diversity happen at GE. Anybody who believes that has missed the boat. White males must be included and must be empowered in this whole effort. In many instances those who are diversity managers are either African-American or women. I am pleased to say that we are now getting some white males as diversity managers.

> When I visit the various businesses, I have discussion meetings with homogeneous groups. More often than not, these have been groups of white males. That has been very useful in two ways. First, it sensitizes me to some of their issues, and, second, it sends a message to them that we care. This is not about white-male bashing.

In addition, like McGrory, Andrews stressed that diversity efforts are integrated with team-development practices. Both see diversity as one way of emphasizing team unity and contributions.

Although most speakers agreed that white men benefit from diversity because it frees them from being clones of one another, there was some controversy as to how best to intervene with them. Specifically, is it possible to create a truly inclusive environment without making white men feel guilty? McGrory believes that the discussion of white guilt should be up front and that white men should not be made to feel guilty.

In contrast, Elsie Cross believes in getting whites to understand how as a group they act as oppressors. She said that understanding an individual's own racism and sexism leads to a better understanding of the systemic issues:

> There is a funny paradox about racism and sexism: If you don't become aware of your own racism and sexism, you don't have the kind of lens needed to look at systems. You have to be able to look at systems and be able to change the way they're implemented but you also have to have the sensitivity and understanding of how you bring racism and sexism to those systems.

With respect to the issue of white men being made to feel guilty or to somehow pay a price for past injustice, the views of participants varied. In the prework poll we asked participants if they agreed with the statement, "It is impossible to create an environment of equal opportunity without having white men pay the price for past injustices." Seventy percent either strongly disagreed or disagreed. Only 16% either agreed or strongly agreed, suggesting there was a portion of conference attendees who felt that diversity interventions cannot proceed without white men somehow paying a price.

Despite differences in diversity intervention strategies, there seemed to be strong agreement that white men play a key role in diversity interventions and are important to their success. In the preconference poll, participants were presented with the statement, "It's too hard to do work on diversity if you're a white man"; 89% of participants strongly disagreed or disagreed.

Several of the resource people suggested that white men are leaders of the efforts. Ted Payne described the various CEOs over the years at Xerox who championed diversity. Gene Andrews mentioned Jack Welch at GE, and Dawn Cross spoke of Jamie Houghton's leadership role at Corning. Similarly, Danelle Scarborough referred to Jack McGrory's strong stance on diversity for the City of San Diego.

Elsie Cross pointed out that it is critical that white men stand up for the issue and that they model appropriate behaviors. For example, she said that women should not always have to say to men, "You interrupted me." Men in a meeting can say, "You interrupted Mary, or I didn't get to hear what she had to say." Similarly, Cross stated that men should take advantage of work-family practices such as paternity leave and shouldn't be shy about saying, "I have to leave at five to pick up my child from day care."

According to Price Cobbs, for a diversity intervention to be successful, the whole organization must understand and embrace it. It has to be seen as a core value that everyone is committed to.

Chapter 3
HOW SHOULD A DIVERSITY INITIATIVE PROCEED?

Assuming an organization has sufficient commitment to begin looking at the issue of diversity, then the next question is how to proceed. Is there an ideal sequence of events that occurs in a diversity effort? Which diversity activities are most important? How should key activities be positioned to have the most impact? What are the critical first steps to take? Let's begin with a fictional scenario that illustrates how perplexing and frustrating these questions can be.

George, president of a $3 billion corporation, is meeting with some of his staff. He explains that he has just completed a two-day retreat with several other board members of another company. The retreat focused on cultural diversity and, by his own admission, he emerged from this "incredible experience" as "a changed man."

This scenario was the basis for a lengthy panel discussion during the conference, in which several people reacted to George's enthusiastic call to make his company a "best-practice" corporation in cultural diversity. Catherine Buntaine, an organizational development consultant who specializes in assisting clients to build high-performing and inclusive workplaces, created this scenario and assumed the role of George as he laid out his plan and sought advice from various staff members:

George: This is my plan, and I'd like to see it rolling out in about thirty days:

It would be a good idea to set about a 50% recruiting target for women and people of color. I'd like to see a recruiting plan that brings in about 50% in each recruiting cycle.

I think we need a one-day training program for everybody in the organization, maybe below director level. Above directors, I think four hours. I went to a two-day program and I'm slow on this stuff, so I think that will do it.

I want to have one of those diversity committees, a kind of task force that is diverse and can provide leadership to this effort. I want it to be a nice diagonal slice, cross functional and all, because I really need some help with the leadership.

What do you think, folks? Do you think we can get this going in thirty days?

Kay Iwata: It's a pretty ambitious plan. I'd like us to talk about how this fits into our overall vision and strategy about who we are as a company. Maybe we need to look at that as our anchor point to launch this effort.

Price Cobbs: George, I'm glad that you're getting on board, but people out there in the organization feel like their plates are full. If you're going to go this fast, I wonder if we're not going to have people thinking that this is just another program.

Jack McGrory: I think this is one of the big issues we're facing in the United States today, but it's one with a real substantial risk. If we fail at this effort, we will alienate a substantial part of our work force. We're going to have to take some time and make sure we have a total organizational commitment to it. I think we need to do a really comprehensive evaluation of what our organization culture is; where are the problems, what is it employees would like to see us do differently, and what direction do we want to move in?

George: Aren't we going to create a lot of expectations? It sounds like a lot of turmoil to me.

Jack McGrory: It probably is. If we're really serious about moving forward and valuing diversity, we're going to be entering into some uncharted waters, and there's going to be some chaos and turmoil. There's going to be some confusion among our employees, but we have to make sure we manage their expectations. We cannot create extremely high expectations or look at this as the flavor-of-the-month program. This is a multi-year commitment.

Price Cobbs: You've got to have diversity as a core value so that people will have some sense of what they're being trained for. To do only the one-day training without really getting some awareness in the organization and a strategy might just lead people to think this is the flavor-of-the-month program.

Kay Iwata: I think that we need to do some assessment work. And I think our emphasis on quality will fold in really well. Those two can be folded in well, so we don't overload people.

Bill Friday: George, what have you got in mind for these people a year after you get them on board? What are you thinking about in terms of their opportunities for self-fulfillment, achievement, access? Numbers are one thing, but maybe you have to think about the individual and who you've already got in the organization who has command power and will have something to do and say about the future of these people we bring in.

Fred Miller: I think the issue is: We must not make diversity marginal. There are more Hispanics in the United States than there are Canadians in Canada. I think we've got to look at that and look at ways of segmenting our marketplace; we need to go back and look at our strategic plan and think about it as it relates to diversity. We have not done that before. We've looked at the average white person in America, and marketed to them.

Price Cobbs: The way you're presenting your plan, I think it might sound like affirmative action. A big thing may be that we have to change the culture, and that's not going to be very easy.

George: This is getting more complicated. Where should we start?

Derald Sue: I would ask you three major questions. Why is it important for our company to integrate more racial and ethnic minorities and women into the work force? If this is important for us, why have these people been unsuccessful? Finally, how long has it taken for this company to develop? We have to identify what things are acting as major barriers to racial and ethnic minorities and women. As you can see, multiculturalism in this company is a long-term, ongoing process. It's a hard task, and it's more than a one-shot, one-day training program.

Gloria Bonilla-Santiago: I agree that we have to assess, and we have to put a committee to work on this. I don't think everybody should be involved right now, running around and saying we're going to change the organization. We need to plan strategically with the leadership of the organization. When we have a plan, we assess. Then we can talk about how we go about changing this, short-term and long-term.

Elsie Cross: I disagree with some of the things I've heard. Unless you're willing to do this work seriously and call it what it is, then I think you're doomed to failure. I'd like to have the language clarified and the goals clear. For instance, if you're going to define the business reasons for doing this work, the next question is, "Why haven't you been able to do it so far?" In other words, "What are the barriers that get in the way of integrating this company appropriately?" Once you look at the answer to that question, I believe you'll find racism, sexism, heterosexism, antisemitism, all that stuff. The next question is: What do you need to learn and who needs to learn what?

George: So you're saying I might need to slow myself down here a little bit. Could we start rolling this out next month, and design our assessment, and discover our business case—can we do those things together?

George came into this meeting as a champion of cultural diversity and he hit a wall: his staff. Now they can't agree on an alternative. Some would argue that this is a typical situation, one which keeps many organizations from making headway. Others would argue that this is the first conversation that should take place in any meaningful diversity effort. The question, however, remains: How can George, or any other executive, effectively handle the painstaking process of developing diversity in his organization?

Ted Payne likened the Xerox diversity initiative to "building a 747 in flight." Regardless of what provokes the effort in the first place, work must take place while other events are happening around you, sometimes confusing and interfering with what you are trying to accomplish. Some resource people in the process of engineering their organization's diversity initiative indicated that they lived amid chaos for awhile, that they took two steps backward for every three ahead, and that they were often intimidated by the magnitude of their mission. Danelle Scarborough, one of the leaders of the City of San Diego's diversity initiative, commented that she didn't realize the scope of the task until she went through three or four personal growth seminars on diversity. She came to understand the difficulty of the changes needed, and she also recognized how important it is for the project leaders and diversity champions to be the best role models around in fostering diversity.

Organizations have proceeded to tackle diversity in a variety of ways. For example, Gene Andrews described the process used at GE as beginning with a "best practices survey" of nine companies. This effort was launched in 1990 after the senior human-resource managers and vice presidents of the thirteen GE businesses, along with the corporate human-resource managers, decided to find out what was going on in the corporate world and what the implications were for GE. One recommendation from that research was to establish the position of diversity manager, which Andrews has held since late 1991. Another recommendation was to have a meeting of all the diversity managers from the various GE businesses. The focus of that meeting was defining diversity and developing business-specific strategies. Also, as mentioned above, GE's CEO, Jack Welch, gave a mandate to all of the company's officers at their 1991 annual meeting in which each one was expected to be prepared to explain to him what they had done to advance diversity in their operation by the time of the 1992 meeting. They had a full year to go ahead and take some action.

Sara Lee Hosiery is taking a different approach. In a session led by Kay Iwata and Terri Sligh, Iwata explained that the first phase of the process being used there involves training 11,000 employees in what diversity means at that company. After that, the challenge is to weave the diversity initiative in with a major quality initiative and with some other human-resource initiatives. A uniform assessment tool is being created to assess in all three of these areas, to create baseline data to measure progress, and to identify the kinds of interventions that will be most appropriate. The goal is to get rid of redundancies and mixed messages and have policies that reinforce one another.

Another approach has been used at American Express Travel Related Service, according to Susan Jackson. This approach identifies key business imperatives, links them to strategic human-resource issues, and then considers initiatives to support them. A group of line managers and human resource managers unit analyzed the implications of the changes going on in the work force, and they explored future scenarios such as having trouble attracting and retaining people in a tightening labor market and getting maximum productivity. Perhaps because 80% of employees are women in this business, work and family issues were identified as a major concern, and the group ultimately decided to focus on four possible interventions that addressed these concerns.

These examples show that there are many options in proceeding with a diversity effort. In fact, the array of choices may be a problem.

Too Many Options?

Many managers are discouraged from addressing diversity issues because there are a large number of approaches available. "How should I decide which approach is best?" they ask themselves, sometimes feeling paralyzed until they can discover the best one.

The New Leaders (Morrison, 1992), reporting on interviews with nearly two hundred managers from sixteen organizations, presents fifty-two diversity practices ranked by importance (pp. 292-293). Conference participants were asked in the prework to rank the top ten practices from *The New Leaders* in terms of their effectiveness in developing diversity (see Appendix B). The results are as follows, with the average ranking given in brackets:

1. [1.6] Active intervention by top management.
2. [6.9] Recruiting nontraditional employees at non-managerial levels.
3. [6.7] Employee groups that advocate change.
4. [6.9] Consistent monitoring of statistical representation.
5. [4.1] Including diversity in performance evaluation goals and ratings.
6. [4.6] Including diversity in promotion decisions and criteria.
7. [4.6] Targeting nontraditional employees in the succession-planning process.
8. [4.3] Diversity awareness training programs.
9. [6.2] Employee networks and support groups.
10. [6.9] Work-family policies.

In a discussion at the conference, Dawn Cross noted that participants tended to give a low ranking to some of the practices identified as most important in *The New Leaders*. Although most agreed with the highest ranking (active intervention by top management), as reflected in its average of 1.6, other practices received much lower rankings, including three of the top five.

Thus, participants and the interviewees in *The New Leaders* are consistent in emphasizing the critical role of top management in any diversity initiative, but there seems to be little agreement among participants, and only some agreement with the research results, on the effectiveness of other key diversity tools and techniques. The lack of consensus may be partly because there is no one best way for any organization. As Kay Iwata and Terri Sligh noted, "You begin the journey, and the direction is shaped by the culture and the leaders."

Some of the disagreement, however, may reflect uncertainty on the part of participants about how to go about using these and other practices to achieve their diversity goals. There may be so many options that people feel overwhelmed by them. How does one choose from among all of these possibilities a combination that is right for any particular organization?

The practices with the best chance of success seem to be those that fit the organization's business needs, its culture and values, and the key concerns of employees. Terri Sligh and Kay Iwata explained in their session that, because there are many different possible ways to proceed, ideas must come from a cross-section of employees; thus, the leaders are seen as being committed to employees' needs and goals. It is important to incorporate employee input, via focus groups and surveys, into any plan.

Other practitioners make it a point to link the diversity initiative with key organizational values. GE, for example, connects diversity to their eight corporate values, especially the one that involves leaders who build and maintain high-performing diverse teams and the one that concerns involvement of all employees in the business.

Corning, like many other organizations, has tied diversity to its total quality management (TQM) initiative, which was begun several years before the diversity effort. The TQM initiative represents a key building block for diversity, according to Dawn Cross, because it showed how the quality of people is a business issue, and it provided tools and a language that have been extended to the diversity effort. The employee teams formed to address diversity issues within Corning, for example, are termed "Quality Improvement Teams."

The connection between quality and diversity is one of the most obvious to many managers. Most of the participants indicated on the prework that they agree (47%) or strongly agree (31%) with the statement that "Organizations that don't tie diversity into a total quality management initiative are making a big mistake." To the extent that the quality initiative is credible and effective, the link with diversity can be a significant building block. Bob Davis noted that interest in this link is so great that the Institute for Managing Diversity is developing a seminar on it. "Managing diversity," he noted in his session, "is a facilitator for total quality and other large-scale change initiatives."

As we have seen, connecting diversity with an organization's goals, values, and complementary activities is a way to get it ingrained in the system. Tying diversity to the business strategy was particularly recommended by a number of resource people at the conference. The diversity initiative itself, however, also needs a strategy of its own to be effective. One of the recommendations in *The New Leaders* is to use a three-pronged strategy that balances activities oriented toward (1) educating employees; (2) enforcement or holding employees accountable for diversity goals; and (3) exposing employees to "different" people in their work.

The education process and accountability techniques will be discussed in some detail below. The element of exposure, which often involves recruitment tools and techniques used in organizations, is needed to give managers and other employees personal experience working side-by-side with nontraditional colleagues. This experience complements their conceptual knowledge about diversity and helps break down stereotypes that still persist in business and in society overall.

Exposure is not always effective, however. Derald Sue outlined four conditions needed for exposure to be an effective element: commitment from the top; equal status; mutually shared goals; and rewards. Tailoring recruitment practices to help satisfy these conditions will help ensure a balanced strategy.

The range of diversity practices may seem limitless at times, but keeping this three-part strategy in mind will help when it comes time to choose some promising practices over others.

Must "Awareness" Be the First Step?

Take a minute to read the following scenario and answer the questions posed.

Jack argues that diversity activities are doomed until prejudice is addressed. He insists that diversity-awareness training must be completed before other diversity practices are adopted. Jill counters that prejudice is so strong and pervasive that even a five-day training program will have little if any impact. She objects to spending money on training and instead recommends making changes in the performance evaluation and promotion systems.

Do you agree more with Jack or Jill? Why?

Do you think training is the most effective way to combat prejudice? Are there other strategies that you have found to be more effective?

These questions were presented to the conference participants as part of their prework. Participants' responses, and the discussions that took place during the conference, suggest how difficult it is for practitioners to get a hold on diversity issues and, with confidence, take the first step forward.

Nearly half of the 104 participants who answered the first question sided with Jack. Their reasons include:

(1) People need to understand their own attitudes, beliefs, and behaviors before they can accept and support any systemic changes around diversity.

(2) I believe that change of this magnitude must begin with awareness, not new structures. Education done properly will affect the culture, and the structures/systems change will follow more effectively.

(3) Jill's attitude is negative, arbitrary, and completely insensitive to feelings and attitudes that are at the core of diversity dynamics.

(4) Many people have good intentions and are willing to learn about how they can contribute more to a rich work environment and their company's goals. They should not be denied the opportunity to learn how to remove old symbols that perpetuate prejudice, and this learning is a critical first step in removing prejudice. Punishment has been used unsuccessfully in the past.

(5) In my experience, even behavior changes do not last without awareness and some knowledge as to why the behaviors (or evaluations, promotions, etc.) need to change. Most people think they aren't prejudiced and therefore don't even reflect on the problems.

(6) Jack wants to make the patient whole. Jill want to put a band-aid on the wound.

Elsie Cross is one of the participants who strongly advocates awareness training as a first step in a diversity effort, particularly for top management. In her work with a pharmaceutical company, she put top management through twenty-nine days of training in five years. She sees awareness training, or unfreezing, as a beginning of the long-term strategic process needed for meaningful change.

In one exercise that she used to train managers, she made them aware that corporate policies themselves are often not the problem; the problem is how those policies are implemented by managers. A videotape illustrating the company's performance-appraisal process was shown, and managers were asked to stop the tape when they saw evidence of bias or prejudice. There were two or three stops just within the first couple of minutes, and the managers talked about biases that took the form of racism. As the tape went on, the stops got to be so numerous that the exercise had to be stopped. Elsie Cross was gratified that "they got it and began to talk about it."

Fred Miller agrees that top management must undergo awareness training, and he recommends a full thirteen days. He and Elsie Cross are more

inclined than many other consultants to be blunt about what confronts executives—for instance, racism and sexism—and to not always use euphemisms
to describe problems. Both, for example, often prefer "oppression" to "prejudice," and Miller noted that "diversity is not a program; it is a revolution."
Others said they fear that such potentially confrontive terms will alienate
senior executives, and they questioned whether the client's readiness to face
the issues head-on shouldn't be taken into account in designing the training.

Price Cobbs is another who argued that awareness among the leaders
has to be the first goal of a diversity initiative. This requires that they intro-
spect at the personal level about their whiteness and what differences mean in
general, and it is particularly difficult to pull off because such introspection is
not typically encouraged or rewarded in business—that is, it is probably not
how they got to be the organization's leaders in the first place. Cobbs calls
this process "peeling the onion," because "we mistake our conscious intentions for the necessary psychological work to get there." He argues that
awareness at the top is critical because diversity has to be value-driven to
succeed. Other participants, however, are not so convinced that awareness
training, even at the top levels, is a good investment. In contrast to the fifty
people who supported Jack, thirty-nine argued for Jill's approach. Some of
their comments in the prework are:

(1) There was a time when I definitely would have advocated Jack's
position. However, as I have "moved up" in the organization and witnessed
what really goes on when people decisions are made, I am even more convinced that change needs to occur on a systemic level. Attitudes and prejudice
will take eons to change. We can't afford to wait that long.

(2) Until people must deal with minorities as equals they will not
choose to (most often, anyway). Fair performance evaluation and promotions
help to force the issues. It is like dressing up if you haven't taken a bath. It
only looks okay. But if you go below the surface, it isn't good.

(3) Affirmative action strategies, if positioned correctly, can set the
stage for diversity efforts. Diversity has to *exist* before training on how to
manage it is offered.

(4) It is more important to modify behaviors than attitudes because
(a) modifying behaviors can contribute to and facilitate changes in attitudes,
(b) changing attitudes is a very long and time-consuming process, and
(c) creating systems that are fair and equitable should be done immediately,
regardless of people's attitudes.

(5) I believe that training is only part of the equation and you will never
change some people's feelings. However, if you have the systems in place to

deal with performance and upward mobility issues, you can change the organization.

The discussions during the conference sometimes became intense:

Participant: I think it is a mistake to try to change everything, because you can't. "Desegregation" is a powerful symbolic word, because what it says is that the system was one of segregation. And we can't go from a system of segregation to a system of integration without the intermediate step of a system of desegregation. I think that is where we are with organizations right now. You bring more diversity into the organization and this will in itself bring about the change.

Elsie Cross: I wish you were right, but let me tell you that one of the other things that organizations I consult with are dealing with is called the "revolving door syndrome." In good times nontraditionals are gone. They also drop out on the job. I think there has to be a transitional place where you do begin changing part of the culture. This is a social system, and it takes a lot of work. I believe that the people who are going to change it most are the people who own it. And having them acknowledge that we are actually part of the power is very difficult work. That is what we are about.

Ann Morrison took issue with Elsie Cross's position during a session on how training fits into a diversity initiative. While Cross recommended a three- to five-day training program to help executives "unfreeze" and change their mindsets, Morrison argued that training should support system changes and new, explicit behavioral expectations of managers. Several practitioners explained in other sessions that training had not been effective. Dawn Cross, for example, noted that one mistake made at Corning was to start awareness training separately; they couldn't tell people what to do differently, and there was no skill training involved. "We lost momentum," she lamented. Ted Payne also acknowledged that mistake at Xerox. "They just ran off and created a training program," he commented. "We thought a day and a half of training would purge the biases of white male managers." One complication at Xerox, however, was that the trainers were not adequately skilled to handle the training effort, according to Payne; they were internal staff members from the affirmative action department.

The many pitfalls associated with diversity awareness training apparently made some participants wary of putting it as the first step. So many things can go wrong and cause problems for an organization. Danelle Scarborough mentioned that the first pilot training program for city employees of San Diego bombed because they didn't pay enough attention to the psychological dynamics that participants experience. Susan Jackson also noted a few pitfalls. Nontraditionals complain that training seems to reinforce stereotypes; legal liability may be involved when biases are revealed in a training session; people go into programs with great expectations of changing the world quickly, yet they are afraid to collect data on how effective the training was.

Some participants believe that the value of training is suspect, and that there are other, better ways to combat prejudice. Only 32% of the participants, for example, agreed with the statement, "Training is probably the most effective way to combat prejudice." To increase awareness of problems and prejudices, alternative techniques were suggested. A frequent suggestion was to conduct an organizational assessment and to get the results to top management. Bob Davis recommended doing an audit to get at the roots of the organization's culture and then showing senior managers how these roots affect business practices and behaviors. He noted that when top management is presented with the assessment results, their typical initial reaction is denial. "But we've planted the seeds and a model," he continues, "and eventually, they come back to us feeling committed." Until that happens, Davis feels that training is futile.

Many others at the conference shared Davis's view, and some see the assessment findings as a way to shape any training that is eventually done. Ann Morrison proposed a thorough assessment as the first step in her five-step action plan to develop diversity (see Morrison, 1992). She sees it as the foundation for increasing commitment and for designing not only any training that may be done but also the entire mixture of diversity practices specific to a given organization.

Several people suggested that a retreat is a good way to begin a diversity initiative. During a scenario-based panel discussion, for example, Elsie Cross and Jack McGrory suggested that the top-management team take time to create a vision or plan for the organization and to agree on the core values and norms that would comprise that plan. Members of a diverse task force on diversity might be included in that retreat, and it might take on the appearance of awareness training at times as they struggled to become a unified working group. Cross mentioned that assessment data might be useful to have in that planning process.

Kay Iwata pointed out that the assessment results may be only the beginning step in getting "unsanitized information" to executives, to help them understand what employees go through day after day. Because top management tends to get insulated from problems, special techniques may be needed to get them accurate information about diversity issues. Employees who feel that they are being treated unfairly, for example, and attend professional meetings with people of their own sex or ethnic group, may be telling people, "Don't come to work for this organization; this is a very hostile place." These things tend to rock people who are living in an insular world. The focus groups of high-potential employees used at Lockheed represent one way to keep the CEO informed.

Iwata also suggested choosing allies from within the senior-management team—so-called product champions for diversity—to help keep information flowing upward and keep the issues alive. As mentioned earlier, one participant who studied the demographics of the top-management team discovered that one of the more influential executives had five career-oriented daughters who found an ally for diversity in the CEO. Looking for individual executives who have a vested interest in changing the organization can be an effective technique.

Based on all this information, it seems that the argument between Jack and Jill doesn't convey the full picture. The debate is clearly not limited to a question of whether to train or not to train. This choice is too restrictive for some, who argue that it is not an either-or matter. For example, the remaining fifteen respondents who completed the prework refused to choose between the approaches offered by Jack and Jill. Instead, they opted for both or neither, arguing that a combination of the two is essential to develop diversity in an organization. In fact, many of the participants who did feel compelled to choose one or the other approach commented that elements of both should be incorporated into a diversity strategy.

Fewer than a third of the participants agreed with the prework statement, "It's a good idea to do diversity training even if it's clear that an organization does not want to undertake any other diversity activities." And given the chance as a consultant to contract with an organization to train 10,000 employees, many participants noted in the prework that they would first ensure that senior management was committed to diversity, conduct an organizational assessment, or otherwise take steps to ensure that training was not the only activity on the agenda, even though it would be a lucrative contract for them.

From their comments, many participants seemed to have a sense that diversity is both a matter of the heart (related to one's values and ethics) and of the head (a rational way to be competitive in business and get ahead).

Bernardo Ferdman commented in his session on organizational orientations to diversity that it requires "a constant back-and-forth between the overarching values and the policies and procedures to implement them." He thinks that education and reflection are important but that instruments such as evaluation procedures and reward systems must also evolve to facilitate education:

> I think you need to keep working on values. At the same time, the instruments that we use to implement those values have not aligned themselves with the people we're looking for. So people are using the instruments to guide their ideas about what is fair or what isn't, instead of trying to create new instruments to put these new values in place.

Danelle Scarborough agreed that values and business practices need to work in tandem. She said that the consultants working with her on the City of San Diego's diversity initiative told her to wait to change the systems until they changed the employees' "lenses" through educational sessions. But the consultants also recommended some immediate changes that could precede training and get the momentum going. These changes included diversifying the hiring panels, publishing job-transfer (as well as promotion) opportunities, and giving out a phone number that would provide employees with information about the rights and resources available to them.

Training may be a way to change attitudes, to get people psychologically and emotionally on board for the lengthy change process; some participants, however, felt that other activities could be at least as effective as training in achieving this. Giving managers and other employees more exposure in work relationships with people who are different from them was one frequently mentioned strategy; another was giving managers more accountability for their behavior and results concerning developing diversity.

What should you do first? It may be a matter of getting your foot into any door that is ajar. If assessment data can be collected, use it to get the attention and commitment of top management. If training appears to be a promising vehicle to build awareness, do that. If a planning retreat can be arranged, jump on that. Tie diversity goals to other key objectives and activities of the organization. Use whatever is available in the way of resources and connections to begin, rather than waiting for the perfect situation. The first step is the hardest, and one of the most critical. Considerable thought should be given to the first step, but something done imperfectly is usually more effective than nothing done at all.

How Critical Is Accountability, and How Can It Be Built Into a Diversity Effort?

In Elsie Cross's session on "Philosophy and Definition of Managing Diversity," one participant lamented that, despite all the sensitivity training that had gone on in his R&D organization,

> There has not been any real impact. We've done a fantastic job of recruiting, but we bring people in and pretty much they're stuck at the bottom. . . . We feel some perception that if you have too many minorities and women at the top, you won't be seen as one of the leading-edge R&D companies. We have a program for everything you have mentioned, but we don't see results . . . . I think it boils down to accountability.

Cross had elaborated on accountability earlier in this session. She explained that in one of her client companies, the president finally resorted to holding his managers accountable after working on diversity issues for about seven years:

> The president said, "I will train you; I will support you; I will send you all to get more training. But if you cannot manage in a diverse work force, well, you don't belong here." He fired two white men because they couldn't get it. He gave them seven years to get it. I think that is a long time.

Some people feel the need to avoid accountability because it smacks of affirmative action, Cross acknowledged, but she doesn't view affirmative action as negatively as some do: "I believe anybody who feels that affirmative action didn't work does not know what is going on." Until 1965 (after the Civil Rights Act of 1964), "Organizations didn't hire blacks. I couldn't get a job when I got out of Temple University with a degree in business administration, near the top of my class." Without some pressure or enforcement, Cross contended, the progress already made could not have taken place.

Many other participants agreed with her. In the prework, for example, nearly 60% of the respondents agreed with the statement, "Organizations that hold managers accountable for statistical diversity goals have the best chance of achieving success in developing diversity."

Despite the demographic changes that are forcing employers to hire more nontraditional workers, most participants believe that it takes something more to foster diversity throughout an organization. Another item on the prework, for example, was: "It's just a matter of time until nontraditional employees reach senior management in many organizations." Before the conference, 75% of the participants disagreed with this statement. After the conference, it rose to 80%. Clearly, participants are not assuming that diversity will naturally occur in organizations, even though the changing demographics of the labor force are so visible.

The three-part strategy recommended in *The New Leaders* includes accountability, or enforcement, as one of the three key elements (along with education and exposure). Accountability is seen as a necessary part of any diversity initiative, one that is critical to its overall success. Further, one of the steps in the five-step action model given in the book is "Demand Results," reflecting the need to focus on outcomes achieved as well as good intentions.

If accountability is so critical for diversity, and demanding results means measuring progress, then what is it we should be measuring? A variety of potential indicators of progress were listed in the conference prework for participants to rate in terms of their appropriateness. The indicators, along with participants' average rating on a scale from very inappropriate (1) to very appropriate (5) are:

4.5 Statistical representation at different levels or functions.
4.2 Turnover rates.
4.3 Promotion rates.
4.4 Representation in high-potential programs.
4.1 Representation on replacement charts.
4.2 Worker satisfaction.
3.9 Differentials in compensation.
3.2 Absenteeism.
3.6 Complaint/grievance rate.
3.3 Lawsuits.
3.6 Representation in prestigious outside programs.
4.0 Representation in training/development programs.
3.8 Performance appraisal ratings.
3.9 Employees completing diversity training.
3.7 Number of diversity activities/programs.
4.8 Inclusion of diversity in business strategy/policies.

There was considerable disagreement among participants concerning most of these indicators. In all cases except two, participants used the full range of the scale. That is, almost every indicator was given ratings from "very inappropriate" to "very appropriate." (Only "Statistical representation at different levels or functions" and "Representation on replacement charts" received no "very inappropriate" ratings.)

The lack of agreement on what constitutes progress, and how to measure it, is one reason accountability is often the weak link in diversity initiatives. Choosing desired outcomes and appropriate measures of those outcomes, however, may make the difference between an effective diversity effort and one that is merely well-intentioned. There seem to be several important elements or steps in establishing accountability, including the need to tie accountability into business objectives; set goals that are reasonable and specific; monitor and communicate progress; make sure there are consequences; and institutionalize.

Tie Accountability Into Business Objectives. Building diversity goals into the organization's strategic imperatives (such as those involving cost, innovation, quality, customer service, globalization, and speed) was emphasized by Susan Jackson and a number of other participants. She also pointed out that a diversity initiative must be customized and emerge from the implications of that organization's business strategy; copying another company's diversity activities is not a good bet. Several people mentioned that diversity had been incorporated into their organizations' long-term business plans and strategic-planning processes.

The connection between diversity and business implications gives diversity more credibility among line managers, who are seen as key players in making diversity a reality. The link also helps ensure that diversity goals are integrated into corporate-wide systems, including performance appraisal and compensation. Separating diversity from the more traditional staff units in affirmative action and human resources may also help make the business connection more obvious to managers and other employees.

Several diversity practitioners felt it was an advantage to be dissociated from EEO, which is often viewed as having strictly a compliance function. Danelle Scarborough's position, for example, is separate from the City of San Diego's personnel department (where EEO is housed); her group has a separate identity in the city, yet it also deliberately partners with EEO on certain projects. A reporting relationship outside the human resource function was also touted as an advantage in their work, because diversity managers sometimes have to challenge the way the human resource systems operate and because they feel it is important to put diversity (and other human resource concerns) into the hands of line managers.

Reporting in at a high level is another advantage for diversity practitioners, which gives them more clout in the accountability process. Gene Andrews, for example, reports to the senior vice president of human resources, who reports to the chairman of GE. According to several participants, the more a diversity initiative is seen as a top-down effort, the more it will be related to business goals.

Set Goals That Are Reasonable and Specific. Who sets diversity goals or targets? Dawn Cross explained that targets at Corning used to be set by the human resource staff, and managers complained about them. Starting in 1991, however, managers began setting their own targets. When a manager brings in targets to review, Cross asks him or her to evaluate whether they are reasonable by using the following criterion: Would you be comfortable telling a roomful of women, or blacks, these targets? If they're comfortable, she's comfortable. "That's my measure," she explained.

More and more, line managers are collaborating on the targets themselves, as well as on how to achieve them. Even in a culture that resists accountability, steps can be taken to encourage managers to take responsibility for diversity goals. Danelle Scarborough said that at the City of San Diego, for example, a planning forum is held after educational sessions have been completed to give managers ideas about what they can do to develop diversity in their own units and to help them take action.

Focusing targets on areas of greatest concern or impact is another way to increase effectiveness. The focus groups run at the City of San Diego revealed three key issues, for example, and a task force of about twenty members was formed to deal with each of these: multilingual issues, the promotion process, and career development and mentoring. Targets in these three areas would certainly be appropriate and would probably be viewed as more meaningful than goals in other areas.

Being as specific as possible can also strengthen the goals that are set. Many organizations now go far beyond affirmative-action requirements and measure much more than hiring rates. At Corning, for example, targets are set for the various salary bands, including those at the very top as well as those at the exempt level in general.

There was a great deal of support among the conference participants for setting ambitious and concrete goals. Nearly 90% of the participants agreed before the conference with the statement, "The criteria used to keep or promote employees need to reflect diversity goals." Getting line managers involved in devising the goals and focusing on some key priorities will likely make them meaningful and effective.

Monitor and Communicate Progress. At Xerox the Balanced Workforce System includes numerical targets for the senior-most levels, according to Ted Payne, and progress against these targets is reviewed three times a year. A report goes to the chairman, and a summary report goes from the chairman's office to each division head concerning how well he or she has done.

Dawn Cross at Corning meets with a team of six to eight managers four times a year to review data concerning diversity, to analyze it, and to prepare a report on any disparities noticed by the team. The report goes to about a hundred people. Dawn also meets quarterly with the chairman and his operating committee, and whenever else she needs to, to update them on progress and discuss issues of diversity.

Gene Andrews at GE meets with his boss and colleagues regularly to review the assignments of senior executives. He feels that this helps keep them conscious of issues affecting nontraditional managers. Also, GE's annual manpower-review process, which involves an all-day meeting between the chairman and each senior business leader, includes discussions on progress in the diversity area. According to Andrews, it covers demographics, plans and specific activities regarding diversity initiatives and successes.

U S West conducts a quarterly audit on diversity. Nationwide conducts a general, semiannual employee opinion poll; on a recent poll in which employees were asked to include write-in comments on any subject, 8,000 of their comments had to do with diversity issues.

These are the kinds of techniques being used in organizations to keep managers and other employees focused on diversity targets. Regular forums help managers see diversity as a priority and encourage them to keep working toward goals. Also, reports of successes can be inspirational to managers who want to know whether what they're doing is effective.

Make Sure That There Are Consequences. Corning's statistical goals for diversity are tied to executive compensation. "There is a 10% kicker if they meet their diversity goals," according to Dawn Cross, "and a loss if they miss them."

Managers are busy people, especially in times of downsizing when they often have to pick up work that used to be done by others. Without consequences associated with diversity, it is too easy to let those goals slide. To make the association explicit, some organizations make the link with compensation. Xerox at one time tied diversity to managers' bonuses but has since dropped that practice. Ted Payne explained that diversity issues affected only about 5% of the bonus, yet managers spent so much time debating whether it should be awarded that it wasn't worth keeping. Xerox, however, does tie diversity to the evaluation of a manager's performance. Human resource management accounts for 30% of the evaluation, and up to half of that can be devoted to diversity. Presumably, that piece of the evaluation is related to merit pay.

There are, of course, even more serious consequences that can be tied to the ability of a manager to develop diversity. At Xerox, targets were set specifically for the sales force. These jobs were identified in the company's pivotal job concept, because most of the top managers had come from these jobs. What happened to managers who missed their targets? According to Ted Payne, the first time there was a conversation. The second time they got a warning. The third time they were reassigned where they couldn't impede progress.

Another company that requires accountability for diversity is GE. Gene Andrews said GE's leaders must deliver on financial commitments and share the company's values. Managers need to meet both sets of goals, he explained; it is not OK to meet only the financial commitments and not the goals around values, which include diversity.

Many people favor use of rewards for developing diversity, because they don't like the idea of trying to motivate managers via punishment. Managers and other employees who are struggling to foster diversity are still pioneers in many organizations. Fred Miller urges organizations to reward everyone involved in the change process, not just senior managers, for the risks they are taking in innovating around diversity. "Change often means some people get bloodied and beaten up," he noted, and they need to be recognized to continue their efforts.

Just as diversity goals may be statistical targets or more amorphous things like changing the climate of a business unit, the rewards may be more or less tangible. More pay is not the only tool that can be used to motivate managers, but alternatives need to be meaningful to the individuals. If diversity is important, then the consequences also need to be important to increase the chances of success.

Institutionalize. The personal intervention of top management in encouraging and rewarding diversity is becoming widely recognized as perhaps the single most important ingredient in any diversity effort. If a diversity effort remains dependent on one or a few individuals in senior management, however, it can fall like a house of cards. One participant revealed that, even though the diversity initiative was going well, "Our fear is that when three of the five people on the executive committee retire in 1993, what's going to happen after that?" Getting diversity embedded into the human resource systems and other business procedures is important for long-term impact.

Summary

Addressing all five of the elements just cited requires a variety of formal and informal techniques. As "George" disclosed in the fictional scenario, simply considering nontraditional managers in the succession-planning meeting isn't enough. George himself was surprised at how easy it was to revert to the old ways. "It's pretty amazing," George said. "In that succession-planning meeting we found a way to knock those folks off the list and to push our own kind up." Dana Friedman challenged George to take ownership of that outcome, and to take steps to hold his managers accountable for the part they play in that process. "You're tiptoeing around," she said. "What are you going to do to the people who don't do it right?" George pondered whether he had the right team to carry out his diversity plan. Fred Miller pushed him: "Some of the people who are your friends who you have promoted to the top of the organization may not be the people who can take the organization where it needs to go."

It may be that the team needs to be reconstituted to move the organization toward the vision and to keep diversity as a priority. It may be that opening the succession-planning meeting to a few other people would change the pattern of selection. At Corning, representatives of employee groups sit in on succession planning. At many other organizations, a diversity specialist or a human resource expert is there to help keep executives focused on diversity goals. It may be that the criteria for succession need to be examined, clarified, or revised.

Most likely, a combination of these things will be required. And a combination of things will be required to affect the way promotions are made, the way recruitment is carried out, the way evaluations are conducted, and so on. Without accountability, however, the likelihood is that very little will get done. The outcomes of succession planning and other activities will continue to look very much like they always have.

Chapter 4
WHAT ARE SOME IMPORTANT DIVERSITY PRACTICES?

In the prework, 74% of the participants indicated that they either agreed or strongly agreed with the statement, "At this point, organizations need to do far more to accommodate diverse employees." As discussed in the preceding chapter, promoting awareness training and making systematic changes that establish accountability are two broad strategies for accomplishing more. In addition to looking at a diversity initiative from such a general perspective, participants at the conference also considered numerous specific practices. Among the more prominent of these were the use of mentoring programs, employee groups, layoff criteria during downsizing, and work-family programs.

This section will discuss strengths and weaknesses of these four practices. Our intention is not to recommend these (sometimes controversial) practices but, rather, to inform readers about them and how they might be used.

Mentoring Programs

Mentoring is a practice that many organizations use to foster diversity, either as a stand-alone program or in combination with other initiatives. As pointed out in *The New Leaders* (1992; pp. 41-42), a lack of mentors may be a barrier for nontraditional managers who especially need the guidance, encouragement, and advocacy that developmental relationships can provide. Gloria Bonilla-Santiago (1992) has said that a lack of mentors is a barrier to leadership for Hispanic women.

These relationships have proven important to career development and are useful tools for developing talent that might otherwise be lost or not developed, especially the talent of women and nontraditional managers. In Ann Morrison's address, "The New Leaders," she also noted that poor career development for women and people of color, in particular, can be devastating because they get boxed in at very early stages. They get hired, for example, to jobs where they really aren't expected to move up. So, in the key early stages of a career where they might be ignored and discounted, they don't develop the breadth early on and therefore aren't qualified at a later time.

To offer information on mentoring programs as a developmental tool at the conference, we asked David Thomas, professor of organizational behavior with a particular interest in race relations in organizations, to discuss his and his colleagues' research findings on mentoring (see Thomas, 1989, 1990,

1993; Thomas & Alderfer, 1989; Thomas & Kram, 1988). His session, "Mentoring, Diversity, and Development in Organizations," is the basis for much of the following discussion.

Mentors produce benefits for both the individuals and the organization. People who have had developmental relationships tend to ascend the learning curve more quickly, get help advancing in their careers, feel connected to the organization quicker, and stay longer. Developmental relationships provide support, sponsorship, advocacy, coaching, protection, recognition, exposure and visibility, and challenging work assignments. They may also give the person a sense of acceptance and confirmation, provide counseling, help her or him find a fit in the organization, and provide friendship. Furthermore, interracial and cross-gender developmental relationships can provide insight into race and gender relations.

Mentoring can take place informally or formally. Informal mentoring is a naturally forming relationship between two people. Formal mentoring programs are matching programs, where matches are either assigned or the mentees select their mentor from a list of volunteers. Formal mentoring programs are often established for people new to the organization, for high-potential managers, or for nontraditional managers.

One advantage to formal programs is that they help create relationships that may not occur otherwise. A participant responsible for a mentoring program commented on how people in her organization wanted mentors but were not comfortable developing the relationship on their own. Their formal mentoring program gave them a mechanism for developing relationships.

Gloria Bonilla-Santiago has developed a formal mentoring program for Hispanic women which has recently expanded to include Asian and black women. This program is a variation on the internal mentoring programs seen in many organizations. Bonilla-Santiago is the broker for the program; she seeks funding for the program, identifies companies seeking women for leadership positions, and coordinates a year-long formal preparation that covers everything from skill development to style. The program has placed more than 70 women in its four years of operation and is considered successful.

Race and Gender in Developmental Relationships. Given the many benefits of mentoring or developmental relationships, they can be an effective tool for developing nontraditional managers. Yet Thomas discovered that race and gender influence the access to and the experience of developmental relationships.

By *access*, Thomas means not only whether people have relationships but also where they find them and with whom they find them. In one large organization Thomas studied, over 60% of the people of color reported having some type of developmental relationships with their white colleagues. They tended to be sponsor-protegé relationships, which provide career functions necessary for people to learn their job from a technical standpoint and to advance in their careers.

People of color were also likely to have mentor relationships within their people-of-color networks. These mentor-mentee relationships provided the same career support that is present in sponsor-protegé relationships. Further, they provided psychosocial support that helped people connect with the organization and with their role in it. Psychosocial support requires a deep emotional connection and identification. However, these mentors were often lower in the hierarchy (but with more seniority) than white mentors. So people of color often were not mentored by people who had the influence to get them through the barriers to senior management known as *the glass ceiling*.

In terms of experience, Thomas found that in naturally forming relationships, cross-race and cross-sex mentors provide less psychosocial support than do same-race and same-sex mentors. They tend to provide less of the following: emotional connection and identification; less counseling, acceptance and confirmation; less help finding the person's fit in the organization; and less friendship. Cross-race and cross-sex relationships are less likely to develop into the full relationship that can be critical to advancement in the manager's career.

Full relationships are important because, as you go up the hierarchy, the risk associated with sponsoring people increases. If a job assignment is perceived as having high risk or high visibility, such as a start-from-scratch or a turnaround job, a manager is more likely to promote a person with whom he or she has developed a full relationship. Women and people of color are less likely to be promoted into the high-risk positions since they don't have relationships with the level of comfort that risk-taking requires; there is a lack of emotional attachment (the psychosocial function), and if there is any doubt about the person, the sponsor may not advocate him or her for the promotion. High-risk jobs usually are the type of job assignment that provide opportunities for development and can potentially advance a person's career. Without opportunities for these assignments, white women and people of color are less likely to break the glass ceiling, and organizations tend to lose out on developing talent and increasing diversity at higher levels.

Not only do nontraditional managers have less access to developmental relationships and find there are differences when they do experience them, there are also some perceptions that cross-race and cross-sex relationships are likely to have problems and therefore are not worth the effort. Nevertheless, 94% of the conference respondents agreed with the statement, "Regardless of problems these relationships may encounter, they are well worth the risk." Although we did not capture accounts describing problems with cross-race and cross-sex relationships from our participants, Thomas's experience suggests that there are complexities in such relationships. These intricacies likely prohibit people from taking full advantage of the relationships. The following are some complexities, based on Thomas's research, that may be encountered in cross-race and cross-sex developmental relationships:

(1) There may be negative stereotyping and incorrect assumptions.

(2) There may be collusion in stereotypical roles. Careers of women are often hurt because the relationship assumes a father-daughter dynamic; the "father" protects the "daughter" by not giving her the risky jobs and and not pushing her out early in her career.

(3) If the mentor is a white woman or person of color, the relationship may be less prestigious than one with a white male and it may have relatively less influence on the ultimate success of the mentee.

(4) In cross-sex relationships there may be inhibiting concerns about intimacy and sexuality.

(5) In organizations where there is some racial conflict and where it appears that people of color do not get ahead, there may be discomfort about mentoring across racial lines—is the person of color selling everyone else out?

(6) These relationships receive more public scrutiny than same-race and same-sex relationships.

(7) It may be necessary to discuss taboo subjects (such as sexual attraction or relations) in order for the relationship to move forward.

How can we help managers be prepared to deal with such complexities? We asked this question of conference participants in the prework, and from their answers we identified a number of strategies that fall into four broad categories: communicate and discuss issues; provide education and training; provide resources for support; and constantly examine the relationship.

Communicate and discuss issues. Participants suggested that the mentor and mentee have candid discussions in the beginning of the relationship and maintain open communication throughout. Communication is especially critical when problems begin to surface. Early on, discuss the subtleties of cross-sex and cross-race relationships, and the problems that often occur. It is important for the pair to explore possibilities of differing values, strategic outlooks, and communication styles. This also requires a willingness to listen and share feelings. One participant responded, "They have to be able to talk about it. Awareness of differences and the ability to discuss them to see whether or not they apply to the individuals will help tremendously in establishing a relationship." Another person suggested that they not be afraid to ask dumb questions, such as, "Do you prefer black or African-American?" or "Would you rather be called Ms. or Mrs.?"

Provide education and training. Most people at the conference suggested that mentors and mentees attend training together and that it should be part of the orientation sessions of the mentoring program; but ongoing training is also critical. Training should include things such as learning from role-playing and case studies and practicing skill-building in conflict resolution. Many participants said that offering diversity training is important, and so is sensitivity training to help people become aware of their own attitudes toward sex, race, and understanding others. Training sessions are also excellent opportunities to have discussions to build awareness about the potential rough spots of cross-race and cross-sex relationships and to learn how others deal with these issues. These sessions could provide effective solutions, techniques, and tools for dealing with issues.

Provide resources for support. Conference participants also felt that a good support system is important so mentors and mentees can get advice and counsel throughout their relationship. A support system might include a resource person or a coach, advisory groups, or support groups with cross-sex and cross-race peers. Discussion groups on diversity or mentoring would be another means of support for participants. Professional groups or employee networks may also be a good resource to mentors and mentees.

Constantly examine the relationship. Participants believed that checkpoints should be built into programs (such as a discussion among mentors, mentees, or both) where issues are raised and dealt with. The pair should continuously check for understanding and evaluation of their progress. A program should provide vehicles to accommodate adjustments, such as partnership changes or withdrawal. One participant spoke of having recently taken over a formal mentoring program for high-potential people. The program matched people for four years, and nothing could be done in the cases where the matches weren't compatible or the program wasn't effective; they were stuck with each other. She wanted advice on how to change it to an informal program without making people feel as if senior management and people in the program had failed.

One suggestion was to announce that they were looking at the system with plans to renew it. Have a focus group and learn what worked and what didn't; then make changes based on those learnings. Others suggested that mentoring programs should start off on a trial basis, with the understanding that they can switch partners. Several participants said their programs matched people for short durations, and after the formal period was over, people could renew the relationship on an informal basis if they chose.

Facilitating Developmental Relationships. According to Thomas, organizations can improve the chance of having a successful mentoring program by paying attention to conditions that facilitate developmental relationships for people of color and white women. These conditions may assist naturally forming relationships or formal programs. First, organizations that have development as part of their cultures are more likely to have greater opportunity for developmental relationships. Second, access to nontraditionals in the upper levels of management is also a factor; if nontraditionals are in the higher managerial ranks, naturally recurring relationships are more likely to occur. Employee groups and networks can be used to increase access to women and people of color. For instance, they can help create a list of potential mentors by recommending people who are good developers of others.

Developmental relationships for people of color and white women are also likely to form and be successful in organizations where diversity is valued, in particular by top management. In addition, the relationships are more successful when the program is imbedded in a context where training in managing diversity exists and where diversity interventions focus on issues of development.

A key condition for any mentoring program is education and training that are focused on helping people understand how to build relationships. Mentors and mentees should be in the training together at least a portion of the time, and an early part of the education process must be devoted to establishing clear expectations for the program and the roles that people will serve. Lack of clear expectations may result in one party not seeing the other as committed or as not showing initiative. The more explicit people are about what they would like to have happen, the greater their capacity to work with one another.

Another factor that facilitates developmental relationships is carefully thinking through what groups should be targeted for the programs. Thomas suggests asking the question, "Are you clear about what the goals are?" This helps determine the target population. Often programs are aimed at people early in their career or at high-potential people. For the high-potential programs, mentors should have a sense of the developmental needs of the junior person. When selecting the mentor, you should consider what the high-potential person needs in order to advance to the next level, and who would be an appropriate match for them. If the program is targeting entry-level staff, the program should be for everyone, not just people of color or white women. Many of our resource people warn about designing programs for specific groups. Individuals at different levels have different developmental needs, yet organizations often design programs that may be targeted for a certain group, regardless of the members' level, such as designing one for all blacks in the organization.

Selecting Mentors. Another aspect of a successful mentoring program is careful selection of mentors. Mentoring programs are destined to fail if they include mentors who are not sensitive to issues of nontraditional managers or who have no desire to participate in the program.

In the prework, conference respondents generated an extensive list of critical characteristics of successful mentors. First, the mentor should have an understanding and appreciation of the role and realize its importance to the organization. Understanding that the purpose of the role is to serve as a developer of people is critical. It is also valuable if the mentor once had a mentor; such firsthand experience would help with a developmental relationship. At the least, the person should have knowledge of mentoring and be willing to participate in training. More important, the mentor should volunteer, giving his or her time willingly and generously and not be forced to participate in the program.

Another important factor is that the mentor have experience and a proven track record developing people—and not just white men. The person may have served as a mentor before, or have a track record hiring, promoting, and building teams with nontraditional managers.

Being organizationally savvy is also key. The mentor should know the business and be responsive to organizational change. He or she should understand obstacles and barriers to success for nontraditionals in the organization. A related characteristic is that the person know the politics of the organization.

It's imperative for a cross-race or cross-sex mentor to support the diversity effort and have an awareness of cross-cultural behaviors. The person should know her or his own biases and be willing to work on the "isms." The mentor should also have diverse friendships.

Mentors should be skilled at listening, communicating, giving feedback, coaching, and teaching. Other individual characteristics include self-awareness and valuing continuous self-development and learning. He or she needs to be self-confident, flexible, and open-minded. A good mentor adheres to his or her own belief system. Serving as a mentor often requires a sense of humor, a willingness to take risks, and generosity in giving of self.

Can we use existing assessment tools and techniques to identify individuals best able to mentor nontraditional employees? What are some of the tools? What are other ways to determine if a person had the critical characteristics of good mentors? These were questions we asked of conference participants in the prework.

Based on our review of the data, it appears that if tools and techniques exist, respondents do not perceive them as useful in selecting mentors. Half of the respondents disagreed or strongly disagreed with the statement, "We can use existing assessment tools and techniques to identify individuals best able to mentor nontraditional employees." Almost one-third of the respondents felt neutral. A few who were more likely to agree suggested only three psychological instruments: the Myers-Briggs Type Indicator, Benchmarks®, and SKILLSCOPE®. Some were less specific—"a computerized tool" or "leadership inventories." Another participant suggested using assessment-center data.

Given a lack of tools and techniques, how can we then determine if a person has the characteristics necessary to be a mentor? The most frequent response was to evaluate the candidate's track record. Examine his or her performance evaluations and career history for professional accomplishments; this would help assess the characteristics of organizational savvy and success in the organization. Looking at the person's track record would also allow you to tell if the person is supportive of the organization's diversity effort. Has the candidate been a good developer of nontraditional managers? Does the potential mentor have acceptable hiring practices—is his or her current work group diverse? How many people, especially nontraditional employees, has she or he developed and promoted? Also consider the programs, policies, and types of communications that he or she has used in the organization.

While evaluating the person's track record, you should seek multiple perspectives. Interview a cross-section of people—subordinates, superiors, and peers—to gain a variety of viewpoints. Try to learn what type of reputation this person has for giving feedback to others, being a good listener and communicator, developing others, and working and socializing with diverse people.

Interviewing the candidate was another suggested technique for determining if the candidate possesses the characteristics of a good mentor. After the person understands the role and expectations for being a mentor, interview him or her to determine the level of interest in taking on the role. One suggestion was to present the candidate with the established criteria and ask him or her to give evidence of how they fulfill the characteristics. The interview would be an appropriate time to ascertain the degree of commitment to the role of developing another person and to assess whether the person has the desired characteristics.

Employee Groups

Employee groups are usually formed around demographic characteristics of sex or race—for instance, women's employee groups or groups for blacks, Hispanics, or Asian-Americans. They may also be formed around certain common characteristics such as sexual preference. Early in the conference, we began to hear employee groups referred to by a variety of names: employee networks, caucus groups, coalitions, resource groups, employee associations, panels, and forums.

There are subtle differences among these groups in their purposes, how they are structured, and how they function. Employee groups tend to start as forums for support. They are an opportunity for people to share organizational information, to gain access to others who may serve as cheerleaders, advisers, or provide expertise or resources. As networks, employee groups may provide members visibility to senior managers who may later be instrumental in advancing their careers. The groups may sponsor workshops in skill areas or professional-development programs like coaching or mentoring, or they may host and publicize festivities to celebrate their cultural heritage.

Employee groups are a means for people to "cluster," a concept Derald Sue described as the forming of groups by people with similar characteristics. He stated that clustering provides "cultural nutrients" for members:

> All groups, all cultures have a need to practice and rehearse their culture. Especially with racial and ethnic minorities in the work force in institutions that are primarily white in orientation, there is a chronic sense of invalidation that occurs. It's an important issue that we cluster for validation.

At the conference, a white man who witnessed clustering at dinner in the hotel restaurant expressed his surprise; he expected more mixing at a diversity conference. Several female group members (a Latina and two blacks) expressed their need to be with others like themselves after spending their entire work day, and much of their social time, with people who are different. The white man admitted that at first he was angry and disillusioned, but hearing their explanation helped him understand the dynamic of clustering.

Sometimes employee groups form because of hostile work environments. According to Ted Payne, at Xerox Corporation black employees formed caucus groups after they were brought into environments that were not prepared for their entry. A remark by Derald Sue may explain this:

> When groups perceive they're in a hostile environment, they cling on more tenaciously to what they consider to be important. If we allow people to cluster—to practice and rehearse their culture—I believe that they are more prone to reach out.

Twenty years after their formation, the caucus groups at Xerox are still a vital part of the organization's culture. Ted Payne said that when they were formed the groups "helped those early pioneers to be effective in the environment. Where they did not have outreach from the employees who were largely white, they had to reach to each other."

Often employee groups become advocacy groups—vehicles for employee involvement in the organization's diversity effort where groups of employees act as lobbyists for better treatment. Internal advocacy groups can be helpful to the organization because they can be used as a sounding board for proposed policies or actions. Some groups have direct access to senior management, which gives them power; they are often privy to information such as developments in the organization, position openings, or personnel profiles. One conference participant said that groups in her organization (known internally as *resource groups*) have representatives that meet with the company's officers quarterly so that the concerns of those groups are brought to the executive level. For example, a group may believe that in certain areas of the organization Hispanics are not being recognized enough, so this issue is raised with senior management.

This same woman relayed how helpful the resource groups are in her position as manager of equal employment opportunity and affirmative action. If she gets calls from employees who are having problems and are in need of guidance or mentoring, she refers them to the resource group for assistance. If an employee feels he or she has been mistreated but the claim is not considered discrimination, employees often prefer hearing the explanation from a member of the resource group instead of her.

Although there is much value in employee and advocacy groups, not everyone has positive perceptions of them. To begin with, there seems to be anxiety around the notion of employees banding together: There is a fear of employee groups becoming advocacy groups and being demanding of management. Danelle Scarborough described the city's experience with homogeneous focus groups in the initial stages of implementing their diversity effort:

> We were afraid that these would become gripe sessions and explode all over the organization, and that's not what happened at all. First and foremost, it was an intervention in itself because what the organization was saying was that it's okay for you to acknowledge that you have something in common. For many of the groups it was a sense of comfort and camaraderie and connectedness; they were powerful meetings.

> Prior to this point I think there would have been a lot of distrust and fear by having these groups go off by themselves and talk. As a result of the gay and lesbian focus group, the Gay and Lesbian Employee Association was formed. Now it's an association that has grown in membership and has become a powerful advocate group in the city.

Dawn Cross and participants in her session talked about their apprehension of employee groups. She said:

> People are not going to shoot themselves in the foot for the most part. They're not going to destroy their careers and in all probability they're going to come at this with a very responsible point of view, despite being frustrated or angry. That's been my experience. Now, they don't always do it in a way that makes other people comfortable, nor should they.

One participant recounted:

> That's the dilemma right there. I'm not sure the culture of the organization—we're just coming into this—is ready for that.

To which Dawn Cross then said,

> I know that, but if people are angry then someone should know they're angry. I don't think someone should have to temper their anger just to make someone comfortable.

The participant answered,

> I know. Our women are speaking up because they see the ceiling. They
> see that we haven't groomed them inside so we're looking outside.

Often employee groups try to be helpful to the organization, but in their
eagerness to help, they can create dilemmas and tension for others. The
following scenario from the conference prework exemplifies the predica-
ments that might result from a proposal by a black-employee group submitted
to senior management:

> You are president of a company. You have been thinking for the past
> few months that you should be doing something to develop diversity
> within the company, but you haven't yet decided what. Two officers of
> the black-employee group come to you requesting your support for a
> new development program for black supervisors in the company. The
> cost to the company would be quite reasonable, and there aren't any
> formal development programs at all in the company now. The officers
> remind you that there are only a handful of black managers in upper
> management. What do you do?

If senior management supports this plan, will it create problems because
it is for a specific group? Will the program develop separateness instead of
diversity? Will others think the black-employee group is getting preferential
treatment? These are some of the dilemmas that top management will have to
struggle with. Although the employee group perceives this program as an
opportunity to implement a development program for blacks, prework respondents consider this a much broader issue. Underrepresentation in top management and development of employees are the larger issues. Are there other
groups not represented? If not, why? Does the organization have a comprehensive development program for all employees? Organizations should
consider an effort in which development programs are one of many efforts
integrated into a larger diversity initiative. Below are some of the responses to
the scenario from conference participants:

> Advise the officers of the black-employee group that you want to put
> together a comprehensive strategy that addresses the diverse employee
> population. In order to do so, you want to put together a diverse com-
> mittee to: (1) identify the business implications of a diverse work force;

(2) gather information regarding work-force demographics; (3) conduct an audit to surface the workplace issues as seen by blacks, whites, males, females, working parents, and other stratifications; and (4) put together a ninety-day implementation plan. Assure the black officers that you are committed to enhancing the potential of all employees and that you will start by asking for a representative to sit on the committee.

I have trouble with creating a program for one specific area—black supervision. I would work at integrating this focus into an existing continuation or create a whole new one. This proposal does not develop diversity but separateness.

Need to know what the actual culture is. Will such a program be resented by whites and create more problems, making it more difficult to promote minorities in the future?

If there are not development programs at all, then a program for blacks only is likely to prove so threatening to whites that diversity development and, in fact, intracompany cooperation can be severely undermined. Rather, start a developmental program and heavily recruit blacks and other people of color and seek additional training opportunities in the community.

This scenario raises the issue of exclusivity of employee groups. Groups open to only one ethnicity may be seen as engaging in fragmentation, which could lead to infighting. This becomes divisive to nontraditional employees as a whole and potentially destructive to diversity efforts. Ginger Lapid-Bogda described her work with a large women's network at The Procter & Gamble Company. Networks in general, she said, are complex groups:

> Most of the time you find women's networks in organizations end up being primarily white, professional women's networks. I think that's very exclusive and really doesn't help what we're doing with diversity.

A participant in charge of a diversity effort explained that their groups have one rule: They have to be open groups. Once they had an employee group that tried to be closed to people who didn't have a certain characteristic, but the organization told them they would not support that type of segregation. White men may also consider themselves excluded by employee groups. Another participant had a colleague petition to have a white male coalition recognized, but the organization chose not to recognize it.

Several participants discussed the dilemmas that their organizations were having with advocacy groups that formed on their own, outside of the organization. These groups do not have formal ties to the organization. These participants' concern is that such groups aren't being used to their potential, and they do not see positive results from them. One woman said her organization's groups exist more for purposes of visibility, or "fluff," than for action, and she thinks that they have become too entwined in politics. She gave examples:

> If you are president of one of those groups, you are going to get promoted. The leadership thing, it becomes more divisive so far as I view it. I don't know how to impact it. I was in the EEO Office and I should have been the person that one of those groups was dealing with, and she only wanted to deal with the head of the office; she wouldn't even talk to me.

Participants helped this woman realize that without the formal ties, there is no understanding of roles and no boundaries for the groups, and this limits the constructive ways the groups and the organization can work together.

Layoff Criteria During Downsizing

Recent changes in layoff policies that call for retaining more nontraditional managers have sparked a tremendous amount of debate. Corporations cite business necessity as the main reason for policy change: maintaining the competitive advantage in a demographically shifting marketplace and avoiding job-bias litigation (Lopez, 1992). Many organizations now realize that past layoff policy has disproportionately affected women and people of color. For some, this change from the traditional "first hired, last fired" approach to layoffs is a reflection of their commitment to diversity by maintaining the demographic representation they have strived to accomplish. Ted Payne's account of Xerox's pledge to not lose the gains it had made in the representation of white women, people of color, people over the age of forty, and people with disabilities in their downsizing in the 1980s is an excellent example of this commitment.

These changes have been controversial and risky. Backlash and reverse discrimination lawsuits are potential outcomes. White men with more seniority feel cheated and victimized, and they fear there is no one looking out for them. Some conference participants argued that if all managers were being measured against the same performance criteria, then white men should not feel mistreated. Yet they agreed that for many white men this perception will be a reality, so it must be acknowledged and appropriately treated.

Are these policy changes appropriate? Should diversity continue to be a priority when an organization is confronting economic difficulties such as downsizing? Conference participants were asked their opinions on these issues. All but one person responded that diversity should continue to be a priority in troubled times. There was not the same level of agreement, however, on the appropriateness of the policy changes; 18 out of 104 participants felt the changes were not appropriate. The responses of a few of these 18 participants may explain why others also did not agree. One person replied that the revised policy will also lead to litigation. Others said they would not agree with the changes if they create "ugly backlash" or if performance is not considered.

The issue of backlash was addressed in the fictional scenario (discussed in the previous chapter) where "George," a CEO who presents an ambitious diversity plan to his senior managers, invited stakeholders to comment. One replied,

> As a senior union representative on the plant site, given the way the last layoff was handled in which some of our senior union members were laid off to preserve the mix of the employees of the company, and given the history of a sense that this management team has occasionally tried to break the union, we suspect that this diversity effort either consciously or unconsciously is an effort to weaken the union.
>
> We don't see what's in it for us to support your efforts. We see nothing but loss for the majority of our union members. We're not fully trustful of your motivations.

George said,

> Our choice in the recent economic crisis, hostile takeover, and downsizing was not to go back to "first in, last out" but to try to preserve the grounds we've made. I think we learned some things about how we communicated in that process and how we included people in that process. We didn't stay in very close touch with you through that.

That was a tough one and I don't think we've figured everything we need to know about that yet.

Kay Iwata then said,

> If we're trying to skinny down and be more efficient, we as an organization are having to reconsider whether seniority or performance is the factor. When we made those decisions about layoffs they were based on performance and contribution being the factors, and as a side benefit that allowed us to keep more diversity in the organization.

Perceptions of others as a result of the policy changes will undoubtedly stir controversy. White men in particular are likely to feel they are not being treated fairly. In this case, George admitted to the organization that he was not handling the process as well as he could in areas like communicating and including people in the process. Conference participants had several suggestions for handling the backlash that may follow from the policy change, and communication was one of the top recommendations.

Participants felt that top management should outline the policy as early as possible. They should communicate the array of criteria that are being used and explain the rationale from both the business and humanistic standpoints, relating the decisions to the success of the business. One white male participant said,

> I would point out with as much factual information as possible that over the years the system has never been fair, and that policy changes are, in fact, an effort to bring more balance into the system. I would note that white males have consistently been treated as the majority when, in fact, they were a minority. This is a tough task.

Another way to handle backlash is to provide assistance and outplacement to laid-off employees. One person said,

> I would develop support systems and programs for those who may be affected by layoffs, including guidelines on becoming a more effective employee and outplacement support for those laid off.

Holding focus groups to give white men a chance to express their feelings and discuss their concerns may also help.

The fictional scenario led to consideration of another issue: What criteria should be used in deciding whom to lay off? Based on the Xerox case and what we heard during this scenario, seniority is no longer the determining factor. Rather, the criteria are performance, contribution to the organization, and maintaining demographic representation. Conference respondents tended to agree that these criteria should be determinants in layoff decisions rather than the reliance on seniority. The most commonly cited response from participants was that decisions should be based on performance and potential. This participant's response captures the essence of many others:

> Establish the critical strategic developments of the next five to ten years. What are the skills, knowledge, experiences, and competencies required by managers to meet those strategic developments? Choose the managers who are best for the job, given these criteria.

Diversity was also listed as a key factor in the decision making. Usually diversity was suggested as a criterion to use with others, such as performance and potential, but occasionally respondents thought it should be the sole consideration in deciding whom to lay off. One participant recommended a multicriteria approach "which includes reviewing all managers through a screen for future business objectives: performance, potential, ability to develop diverse employees and diversity itself." Another person reiterated the business case for using diversity as a deciding factor:

> Know the goals of the organization; know your customers and their expectations. To meet customer needs and expectations and achieve your goals, you stand a better chance through an organization that values diversity versus sameness.

Work-family Practices

Forty-three percent of conference participants agreed with the statement, "The reality in most organizations is that women can't have babies and an executive-level job." Work-family programs may be a means to alleviate this dilemma, but there are potential problems and drawbacks if the programs are not carefully thought through and implemented. High attrition rates among nontraditional managers, costs associated with recruiting and training due to turnover, advancement problems, and the desire to become more family-friendly have sparked organizations to implement work-family programs.

Organizations that have initiated work-family programs have found that they contribute to gains in diversity and the advancement of nontraditional managers as well as increased worker satisfaction. Dana Friedman, in her session on family-friendly companies, said that employees who were taking advantage of work-family programs reported that they give more of themselves and are more productive and trusting.

Organizations often separate work-family programs from diversity initiatives, but Friedman advocated that work-family programs be linked to diversity efforts. She also emphasized the importance of combining training for both because work-family issues are "a part of the whole; they portray how you treat people, what's acceptable, and how you measure performance."

Sixty-five percent of the conference respondents agreed with the statement, "The work-family programs an organization offers represent a good way to assess its commitment to diversity." However, 18% responded neutrally to the item, and 16% either disagreed or strongly disagreed.

There are several types of programs and policies organizations can choose from when developing a work-family initiative. The categories of options that the Families and Work Institute considers when assessing corporate friendliness are: flexible work arrangements, leaves, financial assistance, corporate giving/community service, dependent-care services, management change, and work-family stress management (Galinsky, Friedman, & Hernandez, 1991).

The Challenges. Work-family programs face many challenges. One challenge is that such a program may not be seen as worth the effort of overcoming the barriers that its implementation generates; another is that the barriers may seem insurmountable. There also seems to be a fear of losing control of such programs and not being able to establish boundaries for participants. Typical questions from managers are: "How can we guarantee the client is being served well when our staff are job sharing?" "How can I supervise my staff when I can't see them performing their actual work?" Friedman and others cited additional barriers to increasing flexibility.

Difficulty supervising people working at home. The Families and Work Institute's The Corporate Reference Guide to Work-family Programs (Galinsky et al., 1991) described U S West Communications' experience with overcoming this barrier in their telecommuting program. The organization emphasized,

The practice must be looked at creatively. Supervisors must watch the output of the telecommuters and give help if necessary, dealing with them as individuals and not imposing solutions on them as a group. Telecommuters should be neither rewarded nor penalized; they should receive a fair share of both desirable and undesirable assignments.

Lack of senior-management support. One corporation that Families and Work Institute interviewed stressed the importance of support: "Programs will be successful if management wants them to be. It is imperative that line management be receptive" (Galinsky et al., 1991).

Administering benefits. In most cases, increasing flexibility involves additional costs to the organization in terms of administering the benefit. For instance, if two people are sharing a job, the manager now has two perfor-mance appraisals to conduct instead of one. With the inflated "head count" of part-time workers or job-sharers also comes illusions of decreased productiv-ity. Many organizations are countering this by altering methods of counting staff, for instance, using equivalent staff count (Galinsky et al., 1991).

Skepticism and ignorance of alternate staffing arrangements. In many cases the fear we see of programs is because of people's lack of knowledge and suspicion. Friedman cited the fear of all secretaries leaving at 3:00 p.m. or fear of women on leave not returning to work after their leaves are over.

Equity. Many managers think that equitable means identical, that what you do or offer to one employee you must do or offer to all. In a session, Friedman noted that "the natural by-product of flexibility is discretion." Managers must be comfortable saying yes to one and no to another; many managers are scared to do this and fear lawsuits and other negative repercussions.

Employee abuse. For some people there is the concern that employees participating in the programs will abuse the privileges they receive and take advantage of the benefits. A participant noted that their employees are so appreciative that they don't abuse the system; in fact, she thinks they give even more of themselves.

Other challenges. One participant described the problems her company was having with a pilot program for working at home and job sharing. She attributes the problems to lack of training for the managers. Friedman sug-gested that one way to reduce problems is to have a vision of what it is you want to have happen and what the parameters around the policy are, and communicate this in the training.

Several participants talked about how work-family programs go unused, which becomes another challenge if such programs are going to be success-ful. For instance, Friedman estimated that only 2 to 3% of employees take advantage of financial-assistance programs. Dawn Cross noted that at Corning some employees are reluctant to use some policies because they believe doing so may make a statement about their commitment. During the fictional scenario described above, "George" asked why the men who had had children in the last year didn't use the new paternal leave policy. Their discussion illuminates some reasons employees have for not using work-family programs:

> Price Cobbs: I think, George, it's part of rewarding behavior. It's a great rule, but if we take paternity leave, we really aren't seen as very competitive, and we might even be seen as kind of wimpy, so that until the culture changes and people get rewarded, then we will not see people exercise things like paternity leave.

> Elsie Cross: As long as only women take maternity leave, it will always be seen as a woman's issue and it will always be seen as wimpy and she will not be seen as important. It's when top-level, high-powered managers take paternity leave when a child is born that it will become institutionalized and seen as okay. That sets the pattern for the other men in the organization to have it be okay to take paternity leave.

In Elsie Cross's session on the philosophy and definition of managing diversity she described a similar situation at a pharmaceutical company when they were integrating work-family issues into their diversity process. They discovered "the parking lot syndrome," where managers don't leave work in the evening until they check the parking lot to see whether their bosses have left for the day. People would come to work at seven in the morning to attend a meeting, and leave after their six o'clock evening meeting was over. In their action plans they established the policy of having meetings at 9:00 a.m., 4:00 p.m., or 5:00 p.m. For people who had work and family issues, like child-care responsibilities, it became acceptable to leave. They found that the men who had child-care responsibilities had been ashamed to admit it, but with this policy it freed up people to do a variety of things related to family.

What Can Help? Modelling and rewarding desirable behavior by top management is critical to the program's success. Managers also need to be careful about sending mixed messages when they reward employees. Friedman relayed a story about a company that was just beginning to implement a work-family program. At the company's employee awards and recognition banquet, a manager gave an award to the outstanding employee of the year. The manager described how the employee "stayed all night and worked all weekend." It is clear, in this case, that if a person wants to be seen as outstanding, he or she won't take advantage of any of the work-family programs. People may not be willing to take the risk of being seen as not committed to their careers and not feeling valued as employees. Mixed messages undermine the programs.

Finally, the message from top management must be consistent and sincere—organizations don't want their existing problems to be the result of their earlier problem-solving. In many cases, flexible work arrangements are a way of institutionalizing the "mommy track," as described by Felice Schwartz (1989) in her article in the *Harvard Business Review*, so organizations must consider what happens to the women who take advantage of longer leaves or part-time work. Do these women get promoted, or do they get derailed? If organizations aren't careful, they could think they are addressing work-and-family issues when in fact they've prevented some of the gains that could be made in diversity and promoting women in the organization.

To incorporate work-family programs, changes in attitudes and values are necessary. Some work-family initiatives are easy to implement, but values must also be present, and getting the values can be much more difficult than the implementation. Friedman has found that organizations often say, "Here are the ten reasons we shouldn't do this." Organizations need the attitude of, "No, we've got to do it, how do we make it happen." This is a big mindshift for a lot of people.

Perhaps our values should reflect that we're being totally inclusive by calling initiatives work-life instead of work-family. Does having work-family initiatives exclude other private-life and home-life issues, such as treating single people with respect and treating families with partners the way we treat other families? For example, if we've implemented sabbaticals and two people ask for a sabbatical, and one of them is to care for a sick mother or a sick child, and the other one is someone who is feeling a lot of stress and he or she wants to fulfill a lifelong dream of climbing the Himalayas, can we accommodate both? Or do we rank the importance of the request and assign the sabbatical to the most deserving? Are all sabbaticals treated equally?

Friedman and many others saw a change in management as the key to changing minds. The evolution of work-family programs is very similar to the evolution of diversity in that EEO and affirmative action were about getting the numbers. In the beginning work-family was, "How many programs do you have?" Both were programmatic issues. Now the measure in diversity is, "What's happening to all these people once you've got them?" And the same is true with work-family. True family-friendliness is not that you have these programs, or even the quality of these programs, it's what happens to the people who use them. If programs are preventing people from getting promoted, causing derailment, or institutionalizing the "mommy track," these are critical problems, and the fundamental ways in which companies think must be changed before these programs can have a positive impact on diversity.

Chapter 5
CONCLUSION: WHAT SHOULD BE DONE NEXT?

Luckily, the purpose of this conference was not to have participants reach agreement on major diversity issues. Clearly, a number of controversies remain unresolved. As this publication indicates, however, there was considerable discussion—and debate—on topics that have significant implications for taking action on diversity. Participants tried to sway their colleagues on some issues and were themselves swayed on others. In some cases, they simply agreed to disagree.

The purpose of the conference was to prompt action. We wanted participants to do something more than increase their awareness of the issues, and something different from what they might have done had they not attended. We believe that important action must occur at several levels: organizational, where teams or systems that affect diversity in one's organization are changed; individual, where people take personal responsibility for making changes or behaving differently; and research, where a knowledge base to encourage and guide action at all levels is generated.

The following examines, at each of these levels, some of our conclusions, along with the next steps that we recommend, some of which have already been taken by participants.

Action at the Organizational Level

Although it remains a controversial issue, after the conference, most participants did tend to agree that racism and sexism have to be primary targets in a diversity initiative and that organizations that hold managers accountable for meeting diversity goals have the best chance for success. The disagreement that exists is probably attributable to the fact that diversity efforts must be tailored to each organization. Context must shape action. In one participant's words, "There is no one answer to how to have a successful diversity program. There are a surprising number of things that you can do to improve the quality of life at work."

That surprising number of things, however, is often an impediment to progress because it overwhelms and intimidates managers who want to proceed with a diversity initiative. There are simply too many options for some managers to feel comfortable moving ahead. That is why *The New Leaders* presented the following five-step action model to help guide diversity activities and assist managers in choosing those that best fit the goals and circumstances in their own organization. (Further assistance for managers may be found in Morrison and Crabtree's [1992] description and analysis of 85 of the most useful works from the diversity literature.)

Step 1: Internal investigation. (Re)discover the problems, strengths, and priorities in your organization.

Step 2: Strengthen top-management commitment. Using data from Step 1 and other information, reinforce senior executives' inclination to take appropriate action.

Step 3: Choose and develop practices. (Re)create a balanced mix of practices to support strategic goals.

Step 4: Demand results. Use statistical and qualitative measures to assess progress against key goals.

Step 5: Use building blocks. Leverage strengths and successes to keep momentum going.

These five steps, which outline a long-term organization-change process, were given to participants in the prework. Those participants responsible for implementing a diversity initiative or program in their organizations were asked to indicate, "At what step is your organization now in its diversity effort, and what is the next step?" Their responses showed that, at the time, most organizations were at Step 1 (34% of 125 respondents) or Step 2 (31%). That came as a surprise to us. Because the conference emphasized taking action "beyond awareness," we expected that most organizations represented would have more experience at Step 3 and beyond.

Perhaps because many participants were just beginning to formulate diversity initiatives for their organizations, they focused their thinking about the next steps needed. In the prework, Step 3 and Step 5 were chosen most often as the next step (30% and 28% of 113 respondents, respectively), with Step 4 a close third (25%). In the poll taken after the conference, many people indicated that they saw Step 2 as a priority. One participant wrote:

I more clearly understand the need to embark on the diversity process carefully and with significant line-management support. My organization has a tendency to implement knee-jerk programs/reactions, and these simply will not work when culture change is what is necessary.

Following are other postconference comments about how what they had learned at the meeting was influencing their approach:

I found myself in an adversarial relationship and about to give up. The conference helped me to identify some positive ways to influence the thinking of top management. It seems to be working.

I led our top-management group to include a specific cultural diversity goal in our formal strategic plan.

I have gotten commitment from top management to support diversity work by sponsoring and supporting a diversity leadership team made up of diverse line and HR people and by focusing succession-and-development discussions on women and people of color.

A number of participants also felt that they needed to get others more involved in the diversity initiative, not only top management but also other line managers, additional human resource staff, and employees in general. They suggested getting involvement through various means, including forming focus groups that could provide some of the assessment data needed; creating task forces and steering committees; incorporating diversity more deliberately into management training; and meeting with opinion leaders in the executive ranks. One participant said:

For one thing, I now realize I must share the responsibility for our diversity efforts. I'm unequipped to do this alone, though I still think it's my responsibility to lead the effort.

Along with their focus on increasing commitment and collaboration, many participants also emphasized the need for more accountability. Tying diversity more closely into the business plan and goals is one suggestion to make enforcement more palatable to top management. Simply being outspoken about demanding results is another technique used by some participants. One said, "Since the conference, I've informed top management, consistently, that this organization cannot separate affirmative action from any successful diversity effort."

It appears that the organizations represented by participants will be taking a more strategic, coherent approach to diversity than before, an approach that we feel has a far better chance of succeeding. Participants were drawn to the principles of long-term change and less likely to focus on particular programs or practices as a solution. Given this, there is no danger that the diversity initiatives in these organizations will be look-alike efforts. We are confident, however, that they will be more effective.

Action at the Individual Level

There was at least as much variety in the views of participants at the individual level as at the organizational level, but two themes stand out. One is the necessity for people to understand the biases and privileges that they themselves bring to their work; the other is to maintain their energy level to deal with the complex, frustrating issues of diversity.

A surprising number of participants were struck during the conference by the notion of prejudice and how pervasive it is in organizations. Many began to reflect on their own values and beliefs, recognizing their importance in doing effective work in this area. For example:

> This work is difficult. It takes constant, vigilant self-examination. I will continue to work on personal growth and awareness around issues of race and gender. And I will seek out opportunities to develop my competency as a responsible and effective consultant.

Consequently, when participants reported the next steps they had taken on a personal level, many referred to what they had been doing to foster their own development. In other words, they acknowledged that, to lead a diversity effort, they had to grow as individuals. Some of their efforts are described in these comments about what they had done differently since the conference:

> I have read and reread some pointed articles about the privileges of white males. I am trying to understand those who propose a militant stance and an uncaring attitude of the polarization they can cause; although I don't agree with their methods, I am beginning to understand their reasons and motivation. I thought I knew prior to the conference, but I found there is a lot to learn in our constantly changing world.

> I think I have paid more attention to the "different equals less" attitude, and have discovered that I am guilty of that belief. I also have come to better understand certain positions or stances (such as why African-Americans are reluctant to invite colleagues to their homes) and am more positively monitoring my response and attitude toward their positions. I am trying harder to manage each subordinate according to his or her needs and specialness, not trying to do everything just the same for all.

> I listen more to white males and their issues, and advocated more on my own behalf for development.

> I have been more aware of my own resistance to some forms of diversity—a sobering experience!

> I continue to consider the privileges I have had because I am a white male. I have shared this learning with other white males in the company.

The struggle to integrate greater diversity into their personal lives and dealings is evident in the many remarks made by participants. Their sense of responsibility in living up to the standards they ask others to meet is not something they take lightly. As champions of diversity, they feel they must also be role models.

The struggle to prod oneself to higher levels, however, is only one small piece in the mission many participants see for themselves. Getting diversity woven into an organization's values and business practices often seems to be an overwhelming task. Burnout is a serious threat for many people. One participant remarked, "I can't understand why it is necessary to work so hard only to accomplish nothing."

The frustration felt by many of the managers, consultants, professors, and researchers who work in the area of diversity is reflected in the responses of conference participants on one item in the prework: "A year from now, where do you think your organization will be in terms of progress on developing diversity?" Fewer than half of the 63 respondents (30) marked the category, "Way ahead." Nearly half (27) marked, "About the same." And for whatever reason, 3 marked, "Behind." Many surely recognize that this is a long-term effort that will not show significant results until perhaps years from now. Even with that knowledge, however, the frustration can become unbearable.

One result of the conference appears to be a renewal of energy for some participants who were feeling somewhat drained and discouraged when they came. Some wrote that they were approaching their work with more passion and creativity. "The conference re-energized me to go forth and do!" Some got ideas during the conference that allowed them to bypass roadblocks that had been troubling them. Others had been prompted to join and share with colleagues, which bolstered their morale. And others seemed to put their successes and their obstacles in a different perspective. One person, for example, simply reinterpreted the challenge:

> I did receive a "boost" of energy that allows me to continue to be a catalyst and to fight the obstacles in the corporate culture head on. I still

experience resistance, but I interpret that to mean that I am asking for an appropriate amount of change.

Whatever else they have done to increase their knowledge and to shape their organizational intervention, some participants clearly put a priority on protecting themselves from burnout: "I have done more to maintain my strength, so that I don't get burned out." Finding ways to control their own vulnerability is a key skill, and it is an area of concern for many who pursue a diversity agenda.

Action at the Research Level

Although there has been much research done on diversity, there are gaps. One involves the question of what measures are appropriate for use in a diversity initiative. If we are to demand results as part of a diversity effort, how should we measure those results?

The research done on diversity has not addressed the process of measuring progress. This is an important gap, because the goals set at the beginning of a diversity intervention ought to specify the measures of success that will be used. Many managers are unsure about what indicators of success can and should be used. In the conference prework, for example, most participants gave short, vague answers to the question, "What indicators of success are you using?" Some typical responses were: "Not there yet." "Too new to measure." "Statistics." "What has been accomplished so far." "Permission to proceed."

The research community could contribute to diversity interventions by examining the kinds of outcomes that best reflect effectiveness at developing diversity, and the measures that best capture those outcomes.

Research to identify measures and tools in particular aspects of diversity work is also needed. For example, we need tools to help identify people capable of serving as mentors (or development partners) in a diverse organization. Even more basic tools are needed to help identify employees who are capable of developing diversity in general, not simply in a mentoring capacity but in other arenas as well. Executives increasingly consider the ability to develop diversity as a leadership requirement, but there is little agreement about how that ability can be measured or developed.

Another important area of needed research is career development for nontraditional managers. Many participants agree that career-development techniques and paths, largely based on traditional managers' experiences and lifestyles, are not appropriate for a more diverse pool of employees. We need a research base to help decide which aspects of existing career-development systems are relevant to this broader group of employees and which need to be replaced. On the same point, some managers argue that most career-development practices are outdated and not appropriate for any employee. If it is indeed time to revamp our approach to career development in general, and management development in particular, what tools and techniques are critical to develop and select the leaders of the future and to help all employees reach their full potential?

Development of other useful tools could also be aided by research. Tools to link diversity with business strategies and goals, for example, would help practitioners create a strong business case for diversity. Tools to link diversity to other initiatives, such as total quality management or customer service, would also help connect and leverage the diversity effort.

Another potential research contribution concerns the nature and conditions of organizational interventions. Existing case studies tend to give a snapshot view at one point in time, even when some historical backdrop is included. Researching the life cycle of a diversity intervention (that is, a longitudinal study) would reveal dynamics and factors that don't usually emerge in a short-term study.

Such long-term research projects would fill in gaps about how diversity evolves in organizations through an organized effort. We would be interested, for example, in readiness factors that make an organization amenable to certain kinds of interventions at certain times. The following kinds of questions need to be addressed: To be most effective, when should focus groups or other data-gathering techniques be used? What needs to happen to prepare an organization to accept changes in the performance evaluation or compensation system? Which practices are most effective for organizations at different points in the change cycle? Are different outcomes or measures appropriate at different stages of a diversity initiative? Answers to questions such as these would help practitioners tailor their diversity efforts, taking into account important contextual factors that may change over time.

Finally, the research community can provide more forums that, like this conference, involve dialog and debate to get below the surface of these complex issues. Involving people in more than "hit and run" presentations is important to help understand what is really being done to develop diversity and what has the greatest chance of success. Forums such as this also encourage collaboration between academic and corporate communities, which helps ensure that whatever research is done will be relevant and credible to those who can put it into action.

Forums that are geared specifically toward defining a research agenda on these issues are also needed. Professional associations such as the Academy of Management have held such sessions. Morehouse College in Atlanta is planning a conference in 1994. These and other meetings give researchers (who are also often consultants) the chance to share their work and explore promising new directions.

We certainly know more now about developing diversity than we did just a year or two ago. But there is much more to learn, and to share, so that more managers and professionals feel confident and comfortable embarking on the mission of developing diversity for themselves and for their organizations. We will continue to be involved in that learning.

References

Adler, N. J. (1991). *International dimensions of organizational behavior* (2nd ed.). Boston: Kent.

Bantel, K. A., & Jackson, S. E. (1989). Top management and innovation in banking: Does the composition of the top team make a difference? *Strategic Management Journal, 10,* 107-124.

Bonilla-Santiago, G. (1992). *Breaking ground and barriers: Hispanic women developing effective leadership.* San Diego: Marin Publications.

Cox, T. (1991). The multicultural organization. *Academy of Management Executive, 5*(2), 34-47.

Galinsky, E., Friedman, D. E., & Hernandez, C. A. (1991). *The corporate reference guide to work-family programs.* New York: Families and Work Institute.

Hacker, A. (1991). *Two nations: Black and white, separate, hostile, unequal.* New York: MacMillan.

Jackson, S. E., & Associates. (1992). *Diversity in the workplace: Human resources initiatives.* New York: Guilford Press.

Jackson, S. E., Brett, J. F., Sessa, V. I., Cooper, D. M., Julin, J. A., & Peyronnin, K. (1991). Some differences make a difference: Individual dissimilarity and group heterogeneity as correlates of recruitment, promotions, and turnover. *Journal of Applied Psychology, 76*(5), 675-689.

Kanter, R. M. (1989). *When giants learn to dance.* New York: Simon and Schuster.

Lapid-Bogda, G. (March 1992). How to win senior management's support for diversity. *AMA*, p. 7.

Lehtinen, J. (1991). Service quality: Multidisciplinary and multinational perspectives: An experimental study of service production processes in different cultures. In S. W. Brown, E. Gummesson, B. Edvardsson, & B. Gustavsson (Eds.), *Service quality: Multidisciplinary and international perspectives.* Lexington, MA: Lexington Books.

Lopez, J. A. (1992, September). Companies alter layoff policies to keep recently hired women and minorities. *The Wall Street Journal*, pp. B1, col. 3, B5, col. 1.

Morrison, A. M. (1992). *The new leaders: Guidelines on leadership diversity in America.* San Francisco: Jossey-Bass.

Morrison, A. M., & Crabtree, K. M. (1992). *Developing diversity in organizations: A digest of selected literature.* Greensboro, NC: Center for Creative Leadership.

Morrison, A. M., White, R. P., & Van Velsor, E. (1992; Updated edition). *Breaking the glass ceiling: Can women reach the top of America's largest corporations?* Reading, MA: Addison-Wesley.

Perlmutter, H. V. (1969). The tortuous evolution of the multinational corporation. *Columbia Journal of World Business, 4,* 9-18.

Thomas, D. A. (1989). Mentoring and irrationality: The role of racial taboos. *Human Resource Management, 28,* 279-290.

Thomas, D. A. (1990). The impact of race on managers' experiences of developmental relationships. *Journal of Organizational Behavior, 11,* 479-492.

Thomas, D. A. (1993). Racial dynamics in cross-race developmental relationships. *Administrative Science Quarterly, 38,* 169-194.

Thomas, D. A., & Alderfer, C. P. (1989). The influence of race on career dynamics: Research and theory in minority career experiences. In M. Arthur, B. Hall, & B. Lawrence (Eds.), *Handbook of career theory,* pp. 133-157. Cambridge: Cambridge University Press.

Thomas, D. A., & Kram, K. (1988). Promoting career enhancing relationships: The role of the human resource professional. In M. London & E. More (Eds.), *Employee career development and the human resource professional,* pp. 49-66. Westport, CT: Green-wood.

Ulrich, D., Halbrook, R., Meder, R., Struchlik, M., & Thorpe, S. (1991). Employee and customer attachment: Synergies for competitive advantage. *Human Resource Planning, 14*(2), 89-103.

Schwartz, F. N. (January-February, 1989). Management women and the new facts of life. *Harvard Business Review.*

Appendix A
CONFERENCE INFORMATION

Participants

The one hundred twenty-two people interested in diversity who participated in the conference fell into three groups. First we had twenty-two resource people who formed the core of the experts who gave formal presentations (biographical information for these people is given below). To get a variety of perspectives on diversity, we invited researchers with noted publications on the topic, external consultants with experience in many different organizations, internal corporate practitioners responsible for implementing diversity interventions, and top executives. Their role was essentially to share what they had learned about diversity interventions, what they did that worked, and what traps to avoid.

In addition to the resource people, we also had a cadre of twelve group facilitators comprised of Center for Creative Leadership employees and outside professionals, who were experienced in conducting small-group discussions on diversity-related topics (their names and affiliations are listed below). They led several discussion groups during the three days of the conference.

Finally, we had eighty-eight registered participants who also brought considerable expertise in the field. In fact, several were drafted during the conference to make informal presentations. They came from a variety of organizations in the business, public, and nonprofit sectors, with the largest number coming from the business sector (61%). The majority of the participants represented the human resource function (54%), with the second largest group (15%) identifying their function as top management. Typical titles were principal consultant, senior vice president and director, and corporate diversity manager.

The average age of participants was forty-four years. They were well-educated, 94% holding a bachelor's degree or higher; 35% percent had master's degrees, and 34% had doctorates.

With respect to sex, 66% of the attendees were women, 34% men. With respect to race, 61% were white, 25% were black, 4% were Asian, 4% were Hispanic, 1.2% were white/other, and 1.2% were other.

Format

A variety of formats were used to foster dialog and debate. (A complete conference schedule is given on pages 100-101.) We began with a large plenary session to introduce the goals and format of the conference. This was followed by a presentation by Ann Morrison called "The New Leaders," which was based on the GOLD (Guidelines on Leadership Diversity) research. This presentation focused on the strategic elements present in the diversity initiatives of best-practice companies (companies noted for their progress in diversity, particularly at the management level). To foster discussion, we invited three resource people (an academic, a consultant, and a human resource practitioner) to comment on the strengths and the areas of controversy in the research.

This was followed by the first of four small discussion sessions. The conference participants were divided into groups of ten, each led by a facilitator. The purpose of the small groups was to give everyone a chance to discuss the conference material in an informal group setting. The first session was dedicated to getting participants familiar with each other and comfortable with discussing the issues.

In the evening of the first day, we had a second plenary session. The goal of the evening was to both demonstrate a diversity intervention technique and to provide entertainment. To this end, the Cornell University Interactive Theatre Ensemble gave a demonstration presentation of how interactive theater has been used in training associated with diversity interventions. Sandra Carrington, the associate director of the troupe, facilitated a discussion that raised issues about prejudice and stereotyping and looked at assumptions about different demographic groups.

The second day focused on specific topics. It was divided into six sessions, three of which were concurrent, in which participants could hear one of the resource people speak about their particular area of expertise. A list of each speaker, his or her background, and the session topic is given below. In a fourth session, the small discussion groups met to discuss and process what was heard earlier in the day.

The fifth session, a plenary meeting, was devoted to a large-panel discussion, the goal of which was to get at the range of opinions represented among the resource people. Twelve resource people participated in a panel as part of a fictional scenario. They were asked to counsel "George," the CEO of a large corporation, who was asking their advice on his plan to introduce and implement a diversity initiative. Catherine Buntaine, who created the scenario, played the role of George. The scenario addressed by the panel covered several stages in the life cycle of a diversity intervention.

The panel discussion was followed by small-group discussions that had two goals: (1) to continue processing issues addressed in the panel, and (2) to get conference attendees' choices for ad hoc sessions on the third and final day. Participants could design the third day by requesting specific speakers or topics.

Two rounds of ad hoc sessions were held on the third day. (The topics covered are listed below.) After the ad hoc sessions, there was a final group discussion for the purpose of going over what was learned or gained from the conference. The conference closed with a large plenary session.

Conference Resource People

Gloria Bonilla-Santiago, Rutgers University

Sunny Bradford, Bogda, Bradford & Associates

Catherine S. Buntaine, The Kaleel Jamison Consulting Group, Inc.

Sandra Carrington, Cornell University

Price M. Cobbs, Pacific Management Systems

Dawn M. Cross, Corning, Inc.

Elsie Y. Cross, Elsie Y. Cross Associates

Bernardo M. Ferdman, California School of Professional Psychology,
San Diego

William C. Friday, William R. Kenan Jr., Fund

Dana E. Friedman, Families and Work Institute

Kay K. Iwata, K. Iwata Associates

Susan E. Jackson, New York University

Allen I. Kraut, Baruch College

Ginger Lapid-Bogda, Bogda, Bradford & Associates

Jack McGrory, City of San Diego

Frederick A. Miller, The Kaleel Jamison Consulting Group, Inc.

Ann M. Morrison, New Leaders Institute

Theodore E. Payne, Xerox Corporation

Danelle Scarborough, City of San Diego

Terri Sligh, Success By Design

Derald Wing Sue, California State University, Hayward

David A. Thomas, Harvard Business School

Biographical Information on Resource People

Gloria Bonilla-Santiago. Dr. Bonilla-Santiago, an associate professor at the Graduate School of Social Work at Rutgers University, is chairperson of the Hispanic Women's Task Force of New Jersey and directs the Center for Strategic Urban Community Leadership at Rutgers. She writes and speaks widely about Hispanic women's issues and does research on migrant workers, especially on migrant women and their lack of leadership in the Hispanic community. She is the author of numerous articles on conditions of Hispanic women in the United States.

Dr. Bonilla-Santiago is the recipient of the 1992 Warren I. Susman Excellence in Teaching Award at Rutgers University. She is a fellow with the National

Hispanic Women Leadership Institute and serves on The National Council of La Raza's Board and on the National Association of Social Workers' Board of Directors. Recently, Dr. Bonilla-Santiago was appointed the state treasurer of the Democratic Party of New Jersey.

Sunny Bradford. Dr. Bradford is an organization effectiveness and change management consultant with Bogda, Bradford & Associates. She has worked with a wide variety of organizations in both the private and nonprofit sectors. For over thirteen years, Dr. Bradford has taught, done research, and consulted in the area of ethnic relations and diversity. She has also designed and conducted organizational assessment processes that clarify work-force diversity issues. An expert in instructional design and delivery, she offers training on diversity, as well as on other management and human resources topics.

Dr. Bradford has given presentations on the topic of diversity for ASTD, the American Management Association, ODN, and other organizations. In addition, she is an associate faculty member of Antioch University. An active member of the American Society for Training and Development, she is also president of the Board of Directors of Los Angeles Organization Development Network, a professional association for organization change consultants.

In 1982, she was awarded a National Endowment for the Humanities Grant to study the interaction of race and gender at the University of California at Santa Cruz.

Catherine S. Buntaine. Ms. Buntaine, a vice president of The Kaleel Jamison Consulting Group, has worked as an organization development consultant since 1979. Her work focuses on assisting corporate, public, and not-for-profit clients in building the strategic foundations critical to supporting high-performing and inclusive workplaces. She has extensive experience in cultural change, strategic planning, and executive-team development. Her current areas of research and interest involve the workplace partnerships of women and men and executive development. She also works on benchmarking, core competencies, and performance incentives regarding cultural diversity.

Through recent consultations, Ms. Buntaine has developed technologies to improve the synthesis of strategic business units following mergers and acquisitions. She is a member of National Training Laboratories (NTL Institute) and the Organization Development Network, and is a lecturer at American University.

Sandra Carrington. Ms. Carrington is associate director of the Cornell Interactive Theatre Ensemble and the ensemble's primary facilitator of training. She was formerly a training specialist in Cornell's Office of Human Resources, where she was responsible for the design and implementation of a variety of departmental training sessions for specific work groups, including workshops in human relations/cultural diversity.

Price M. Cobbs. Dr. Cobbs is an internationally recognized management consultant and a psychiatrist. His clients include government and community agencies, and range from Fortune 500 companies to small businesses. Under his direction, the staff of Pacific Management Systems advises national organizations on leadership development, organizational effectiveness, and multicultural communications and networking.

Through more than twenty years of work in the fields of psychiatry and organizational consulting, Dr. Cobbs has developed a clinical model that can change attitudes and assumptions arising from racial, ethnic, and value differences. He has written several books and articles on race relations. Dr. Cobbs has been a speaker and guest lecturer at leading U.S. colleges and universities and has conducted seminars at the United Nations headquarters in New York. He is a fellow of the American Psychiatric Association and a member of the Institute of Medicine of the National Academy of Sciences, the National Medical Association, and the NAACP.

Dawn M. Cross. Ms. Cross is corporate director of diversity for Corning, Inc. She has worked in the area of organizational behavior and management development for many years. She joined Corning in 1983 as a manager of human resources. In 1987 she became the quality executive for all of the finance and administration staff groups.

Before joining Corning she worked at General Motors Corporation in the International, Fisher Body, Harrison Radiator, and Rochester Products Divisions. In that position, she designed and installed innovative management systems in Europe and the United States.

Ms. Cross was an assistant professor at Ithaca College in the Business School, where she taught personnel and organizational behavior. She has served as a member of the Board of Directors for the Seven Lakes Girl Scouts Council, as a counselor for the Ithaca Rape Crisis Center, and as chair of Corning's Society of Black Professional's Program Committee. Ms. Cross was a founding member of the Association of Black Social Workers and a founding member of the Executive Leadership Council, an organization of the top black American corporate executives.

Elsie Y. Cross. Ms. Cross is president of Elsie Y. Cross Associates, Inc., an organization-development consulting firm since 1972. She has consulted to organizations in Europe, Scandinavia, Africa, and the Caribbean. She has also consulted to government agencies, educational institutions, and with Fortune 500 companies in the pharmaceutical, petro-chemical, financial, communications, and industrial sectors.

She was chairperson of the Board of Directors and is a member of the National Training Laboratories for Applied Behavior Research (NTL Institute).

Bernardo M. Ferdman. Dr. Ferdman is a researcher, professor, and consultant specializing in ethnic and cultural diversity in the workplace. He is currently associate professor in the organizational psychology programs at the California School of Professional Psychology, San Diego. Most recently, he was assistant professor of psychology and of Latin American and Caribbean studies at the State University of New York at Albany, where he taught graduate and undergraduate courses in organizational psychology, diversity in organizations, ethnic relations, Hispanic cultures in the U.S., and group dynamics.

His current research focuses on multicultural awareness in multinational corporations and in multiethnic high schools. Dr. Ferdman is also a consultant with The Kaleel Jamison Consulting Group, Inc., and has worked with a variety of organizations on diversity issues.

Dr. Ferdman currently serves on the Academy of Management's Committee on People of Color, as U.S. national representative for the Interamerican Society of Psychology, and as associate editor of the *Interamerican Psychologist*, the society's newsletter. He is the author of a number of papers on ethnic and multicultural issues and is currently working on a teaching and research resource guide on diversity in organizations.

William C. Friday. Mr. Friday is executive director of The William R. Kenan, Jr., Charitable Trust, and president of The William R. Kenan, Jr., Fund. He is also president emeritus of The University of North Carolina. He is host of a PBS television program, "North Carolina People."

Mr. Friday has been a member of numerous committees, commissions, and boards. Presently, he serves on the American Council on Education Business/Higher Education Forum, Commission on the Future of North Carolina (Chairman), The North Carolina Public Schools Forum, The Task Force on Excellence in Secondary Education in North Carolina, Kathleen Price and Joseph M. Bryan Family Foundation (Trustee), The Knight Foundation Advisory Board, and the North Carolina Institute of Medicine, Health Care Access Forum. He is on the Board of Directors of the Teachers Insurance and Annuity Association—College Retirement Equities Fund, and the Kenan Transport Company, and is chairman of the Board of Governors of the Center for Creative Leadership. He is a fellow of the American Academy of Arts and Sciences and is co-chairman of the Knight Foundation National Commission on Intercollegiate Athletics.

Dana E. Friedman. Dr. Friedman is the co-founder and co-president of the Families and Work Institute, a national, nonprofit organization that conducts research on business, government, and community efforts to help people balance their work and family lives. She designs national research studies, employee needs assessments, human resource strategic plans, and management training programs.

Dr. Friedman was previously a senior research associate at The Conference Board, a nonprofit business think tank, where she created the Work and Family Information Center in 1983. At the Carnegie Corporation of New York she conducted a national study of corporate views on family issues that led to the development of the Board's Information Center. She has been a consultant to major corporations and an advisor to government agencies.

She has published widely on work-family issues and is a board member of the Child Care Action Campaign and Women on the Job.

Kay K. Iwata. Ms. Iwata, formerly president of Pacific Resources Education Programs, Inc. (PREP, Inc.), has been a key creator and driver of its "Managing Diversity and Valuing Differences" diversity education program. She has over twenty years of experience in the fields of management development, training, marketing, finance, and education and currently has her own consulting firm, K. Iwata Associates.

She provides education and skill-building programs focused on diversity, as well as assisting organizations in developing systemic approaches to culture change. Ms. Iwata has developed a seven-phase process for change that incorporates education, assessment, strategic planning, implementation, measurement, evaluations, and continuous improvement.

She was a major contributor to the research for *The New Leaders*, conducted under the auspices of the Center for Creative Leadership. Ms. Iwata has also presented at the American Management Association and the National Diversity Conference. She is a member of the American Institute for Managing Diversity Speakers' Bureau of Morehouse College.

Susan E. Jackson. Dr. Jackson is associate professor of psychology at New York University. Previously she held faculty appointments at the University of Maryland (psychology) and the University of Michigan (management), and has twice been a visiting professor of management at Ecole des Hautes Etudes Commerciales, in France.

She has published over 50 articles and chapters on a variety of topics, including top management team composition, strategic human resource management, job stress and burnout, and organizational approaches to managing workforce diversity. Her work on the topic of diversity emphasizes the importance of linking this issue to the business imperatives of organizations.

An active member of the Academy of Management, she serves as Editor for the *Academy of Management Review* as well as President for the Organizational Behavior Division. She is a Fellow of the Society for Industrial and Organizational Psychology and the American Psychological Association, and serves as a member of the Board of Governors of the Center for Creative Leadership.

Allen I. Kraut. Dr. Kraut is professor of management at Baruch College, The City University of New York, and heads Kraut Associates, a human-resources-management consulting firm specializing in opinion surveys, strategic studies, and management development. His area of special interest is human resource management and the development of strategic personnel practices, especially those affecting a diverse work force.

For much of his professional career, he worked at the IBM Corporation, where he held managerial posts in personnel research and management development. He was manager of personnel research studies on IBM's corporate staff, where he directed major studies of how employees balance work and family life issues. The development and use of employee-opinion surveys is an area of special expertise.

He has published many professional articles on attitude surveys, management assessment, and development and succession planning. He is a fellow of the American Psychological Association and a diplomate of the American Board of Professional Psychology. Dr. Kraut has been an adjunct staff member of the Center for Creative Leadership, conducting seminars on employee-opinion surveys.

Ginger Lapid-Bogda. Dr. Lapid-Bogda of Bogda, Bradford & Associates has been consulting to organizations for over eighteen years in the areas of strategic management of complex change, strategic planning, building teams for high performance, diversity, career development, conflict management, and consulting skills. She has worked in a variety of industries including manufacturing, financial services, health care, retail, entertainment, high technology, and service organizations.

In the area of diversity, she consults on the macro-level, assisting companies in the strategy, design and implementation of diversity change efforts. She also works on the micro-level, consulting to organizations experiencing problems with difficult team or individual issues related to diversity.

She frequently presents for the OD Network, ASTD, and The American Management Association. Her articles have appeared in *The Wall Street Journal* and *HR Focus*, and she has contributed several book chapters on the topics of race and gender. Dr. Lapid-Bogda is on the adjunct faculty of Antioch University, Sonoma State University, and the California School for Professional Psychology.

Jack McGrory. Mr. McGrory is the city manager for the City of San Diego, California. He also teaches at the School of Public Administration at San Diego State University.

He has been with the City of San Diego since 1975. He served in the United States Marine Corps from 1971-1974 and is a lawyer.

In 1992 Mr. McGrory was awarded the San Diego County Peacemaker of the Year Award and the National Leadership Award from Public Technology, Inc.

Frederick A. Miller. Mr. Miller has been president of The Kaleel Jamison Consulting Group since 1985, where he has been involved in a variety of large-systems change efforts in Fortune 100 companies. Mr. Miller is known for his engaging and supportive educational approaches, for consulting partnerships with senior managers, and for innovative cultural change strategies. He has pioneered methodologies for the inclusion of the diverse talents and perspectives of all people in an organization with clients in the United States, Europe, Asia, and the former Soviet Union.

Mr. Miller is a member of the National Training Laboratories for Applied Behavior Research (NTL Institute), where he has served on the Board of Directors. Currently he is a member of the Board of Directors of Ben & Jerry's, Inc., The Living School, The Organization Development Network, and The Institute of Development Research (IDR). He has authored many articles on leadership, cultural diversity, racism, individual and team development, high performance, and the inclusive workplace.

Ann M. Morrison. Ms. Morrison is president of the New Leaders Institute in San Diego, which does leadership-development consulting, presentations, and research with a focus on developing diversity. She is also a senior fellow at the Center for Creative Leadership where she worked from 1974 to 1992 on issues of leadership and executive development, directing large-scale research projects, writing, speaking, and designing training programs. She started the Center's San Diego branch office in 1987.

Ms. Morrison recently led a three-year research project, Guidelines on Leadership Development (GOLD) study, which examined the "best practices" for advancing nontraditional employees in organizations. She has written a number of books and articles on leadership and on diversity issues.

Theodore E. Payne. Mr. Payne is manager of corporate employment and college relations for Xerox Corporation. He is responsible for directing the corporate-employment function to develop policy and provide support to the Xerox operating units in achieving their staffing objectives; establishing and maintaining the corporate-employment function as the competency center and communications network for the employment staffs and college relations liaisons throughout Xerox; and serving as the focal point for establishing and maintaining effective relations with colleges and universities.

Before joining Xerox, Mr. Payne worked in the human resources organization of RCA Corporation as a personnel generalist for nine years. His last position at RCA was manager, employment operations, for the world headquarters in New York City.

Mr. Payne serves on the Board of Directors of the Equal Employment Advisory Council and the Board of Directors of the National Employment Foundation, both of which are based in Washington, D.C.

Danelle Scarborough. Ms. Scarborough is a senior consultant and supervisor with the City of San Diego's Organization Effectiveness Program. She is the project leader for the City's Diversity Commitment, a system-wide change effort. She is also responsible for the Management Academy, San Diego's middle- and upper-level management-development program.

Terri Sligh. Ms. Sligh is the President of Success By Design. She has more than nineteen years of experience in the fields of human resource development and organization development and has successfully designed and implemented interventions for several Fortune 500 companies and professional associations. Most recently she was the manager of workforce diversity for Lockheed Missiles and Space Company, where she developed the blueprint for diversity initiatives.

Ms. Sligh was formerly the national director of professional development for the National Management Association. She currently serves on the Board of Directors for the Palo Alto (California) Mid-Peninsula YWCA. She is a member of the National Association of Female Executives, National Management Association, and the American Society for Training and Development.

She was recognized with a corporate award for her innovation in the design and implementation of the President's Executive Action Council for Managing Diversity.

Derald Wing Sue. Dr. Sue is professor of counseling psychology at California State University–Hayward and a faculty member for the Columbia University Executive Training Programs. He is a licensed psychologist in the State of California and president of his own psychological corporation. His consulting practice encompasses national and international assessment, consultation, and training in multicultural and cross-cultural issues.

Dr. Sue has published numerous journal articles and books in psychology and counseling, especially in the area of cross-cultural communications and minority mental health.

He is active in a number of professional societies including the American Psychological Association (APA), the Association for Counseling and Development, and the Asian-American Psychological Association. He has served as past Chair of APA's historic Committee on the Equality of Opportunity in Psychology, a member of the Minority Fellowship Program, and member of the Board of Social and Ethical Responsibility in Psychology.

David A. Thomas. Dr. Thomas is currently associate professor of organizational behavior and human resource management at the Harvard School of Business Administration, and prior to that was on the faculty of the Wharton School of Finance at the University of Pennsylvania.

His research interests are in the areas of organizational diagnosis and change, group and intergroup relations, career development, and race relations in organizations. Dr. Thomas has written and published several articles related to his research. He has consulted to organizations on issues ranging from organizational design problems and major systems change to career development and leadership training.

He is a member of the Academy of Management, National Training Laboratories for Applied Behavior Research (NTL Institute), and the International Society for the Psychoanalytic Study of Organizations.

Discussion Group Facilitators

Susan W. Dorn, Senior Program Associate, Center for Creative Leadership
Diane Ducat, Professor, La Guardia Community College,
City University of New York
Karen Grabow, Personnel Director, Target Stores
Lily M. Kelly-Radford, Director, Leadership Development Program,
Center for Creative Leadership
Carole A. Leland, Senior Program Associate, Center for Creative Leadership
Karen T. McNeil-Miller, Senior Program Associate,
Center for Creative Leadership
Richard A. Morales, Program Associate, Center for Creative Leadership
Stella M. Nkomo, Associate Professor of Business,
University of North Carolina at Charlotte
Craig S. Smith, Manager, The Looking Glass Program,
Center for Creative Leadership
Joan C. Tavares, Director of Programs, Brussels Branch,
Center for Creative Leadership
Karen Y. Wilson-Starks, Senior Program Associate,
Center for Creative Leadership
Randall P. White, Director, Specialized Client Applications,
Center for Creative Leadership

LEADERSHIP DIVERSITY CONFERENCE:
BEYOND AWARENESS INTO ACTION
Schedule
December 1-3, 1992

December 1

2:30 - 3:20	Opening Activities

3:20 - 5:10   "The New Leaders" Address and Discussion
Presenter: *Ann Morrison*
Discussants: *Dawn Cross, Susan Jackson, Frederick Miller*
Moderator: *Kay Iwata*

5:10 - 6:10   Discussion Group Session

6:10 - 6:45   Social

6:45 - 7:45   Dinner

7:45 - 9:15   Making Diversity Work
Cornell Interactive Theatre Ensemble
Facilitator: *Sandra Carrington*

December 2

8:00 - 9:30   Round I of Concurrent Sessions
Gloria Bonilla-Santiago: "Strategies and Tools for Developing
     Diversity"
Elsie Cross: "Philosophy and Definition of Managing Diversity"
Dana Friedman: "Assessing Corporate Family Friendliness"
Kay Iwata & Terri Sligh: "Best Practices: Leadership Commitment and
     Intervention"
Derald Sue: "Multicultural Organizational Development: Competencies
     for Effective Management"

9:45 - 11:15   Round II of Concurrent Sessions
Bernardo Ferdman: "Organizational Orientations to Diversity:
     Perspectives from Multinational Corporations"
Susan Jackson: "Designing Diversity Initiatives to Meet Strategic
     Imperatives"
Frederick Miller & Catherine Buntaine: "Women and Men Working
     Together: A Partnership Paradigm"
Ted Payne: "A Journey to Work Force 2000"
Danelle Scarborough: "San Diego's Commitment to Diversity"

11:15 - 12:15   Discussion Group Session

12:15 - 1:15   Lunch

1:15 - 2:45   Round III of Concurrent Sessions
Price Cobbs: "Requirements of Diversity Leadership"

> *Sunny Bradford & Ginger Lapid-Bogda*: "Leveraging Diverse Teams for High Performance"
> *Dawn Cross*: "Corning's Diversity Initiative"
> *Allen Kraut*: "Using Research to Frame and Act on Diversity Issues"
> *David Thomas*: "Mentoring, Diversity and Development in Organizations"

3:15 - 5:15   Panel Discussion
Panelists: Gloria Bonilla-Santiago, Price Cobbs, Elsie Cross, Bernardo Ferdman, Bill Friday, Dana Friedman, Kay Iwata, Jack McGrory, Frederick Miller, Ann Morrison, Ted Payne, Derald Sue
Moderator: *Catherine Buntaine*

5:15 - 6:15   Discussion Group Session

December 3

8:00 - 8:30   Plenary session to announce participant-requested ad hoc sessions

8:30 - 10:00   Round I Ad Hoc Sessions

Discussion: "CCL's Diversity Leadership Project: A Focus Group"
Facilitator: *Susan Dorn*

Discussion: "Consultant Exchange Group"
Facilitators: *Elsie Cross and David Thomas*

Panel Discussion: "More from Best Practice Companies"
Panelists: Gene Andrews, Dawn Cross, Ted Payne
Moderator: *Karen Grabow*

Panel Discussion: "Tools for Developing Diversity"
Panelists: Sandra Carrington, Kay Iwata, Danelle Scarborough
Moderator: *Ann Morrison*

Discussion: "Vision & Culture Change"
Moderator: *Bill Drath*

10:15 - 11:45   Round II Ad Hoc Sessions

Price Cobbs: "More from Price Cobbs"
Elsie Cross: "More from Elsie Cross"
Bob Davis: "Concepts from the American Institute for Managing Diversity (Developed by Roosevelt Thomas)"
Ginger Lapid-Bogda: "Top Management Commitment"
David Thomas: "More on Mentoring"

11:45 - 12:45   Lunch

12:45 - 2:15   Discussion Group Session

2:15 - 3:00   Closing Activities

Concurrent Session Descriptions
Leadership Diversity: Beyond Awareness Into Action

ROUND I OF CONCURRENT SESSIONS

Gloria Bonilla-Santiago
Strategies & Tools for Developing Diversity

The focus of Gloria Bonilla-Santiago's workshop was on effective management of diversity, which is a long-term, strategic intervention in organizations. This session explored techniques to ameliorate obstacles and barriers and to bring about basic changes in the organizational culture about the value of differences.

Strategies, tools, and applied research findings for a model of successful intervention in handling diversity among Hispanic women were introduced.

Derald Wing Sue
Multicultural Organizational Development: Competencies for Effective Management

Multicultural organizational development can be described as occurring on two different levels: (a) individual competencies required for the effective management of a diverse labor force and (b) organization movement toward valuing diversity. Culturally competent managers seem to fulfill three criteria: First, they are in the process of becoming more culturally aware of their own values, biases, and assumptions about human behavior in the world of work. Second, they have begun the process of understanding the world view of their culturally diverse work force—their values, biases, and assumptions about human behavior. Third, they have developed a wide repertoire of culturally appropriate and relevant management and communications skills in working with the culturally different worker.

While some discussion was directed toward organizational characteristics needed to become multicultural, this session concentrated mainly on the barriers to effective multicultural management and the beliefs/attitudes, knowledges, and skills required to become a multicultural employee.

Elsie Y. Cross
Philosophy and Definition of Managing Diversity

The focus of Elsie Y. Cross' session was the philosophy and definition of managing diversity. She described the importance of working against the barriers to the full utilization of people of color, white women, and others who have been denied equal opportunity in organizations. The session also focused on the business and professional reasons for managing diversity. Ms. Cross described strategies that address racism and sexism as well as other forms of discrimination at the individual, group, and systemic levels of organizations. Ultimately, all employees, including white men, must benefit from the organizational change effort called managing diversity.

Dana E. Friedman
Assessing Corporate Family Friendliness

This session reviewed the work-family initiatives and environmental factors that characterize "family friendly companies." The speaker reviewed a range of employee needs and current trends among employers to respond to those needs. Based on a study of the largest employers in the country, the presentation included the most popular options and the likely directions for the future.

Discussion also included the obstacles to adopting a work-family agenda and strategies for promoting new work-family initiatives or expanding existing efforts.

Kay K. Iwata & Terri Sligh
Best Practices: Leadership Commitment and Intervention

One of the key "best practices" identified in the Guidelines On Leadership Diversity study was leadership commitment and intervention. This session shared the case study of Lockheed Missiles and Space Company (LMSC) as it developed a top-down approach to their diversity change process. As well as an overall view of the LMSC prototype, participants learned how a typical intervention (education/awareness session) was implemented in a unique way to create a broader cadre of change advocates.

ROUND II OF CONCURRENT SESSIONS

Bernardo M. Ferdman
Organizational Orientations to Diversity: Perspectives from Multinational Corporations

What is the best stance for organizations to take with regards to diversity? To what extent are cultural differences perceived as having a negative impact and as problems to be overcome, and to what extent are they viewed as contributing positively to the firm? Do such perceptions relate to differential practices? Organizations can vary widely in their orientations to cultural diversity. Some organizations do not recognize any impact or relevance of cultural differences, others seek to minimize this impact, and yet others consider it a source of strength. Such alternative visions stem from distinct views regarding the nature and role of cultural differences and can be reflected in organizational aspects of both between- and within-country diversity. Based on data from surveys and interviews of top executives in the Argentine subsidiaries of U.S. companies and the U.S. subsidiaries of Japanese companies, the focus of this session was on both the range of possible and actual orientations to diversity and the connections between these views and other aspects of the organizations, such as decision making, relationships with headquarters, local-expatriate relationships, and personnel selection. Part of the session also was devoted to a discussion of the broader implications of the findings and of linking domestic and international perspectives on diversity.

Theodore E. Payne
A Journey to Work Force 2000

This session provided an overview of the Balanced Workforce Strategy that Xerox employs today, including its origin and how it is maintained. It also examined the key management practices that need to be employed to build and maintain a diverse work force, including top management involvement, establishing goals, communications, and maintaining commitment. The role of managers and employees in a diversity effort was discussed.

Participants learned about the challenges that developed and how they were met, and developed an understanding of the management process used to drive a diversity effort in an organization.

Susan E. Jackson
Designing Diversity Initiatives to Meet Strategic Imperatives

Like all human resources initiatives, diversity initiatives are more likely to enjoy long-term success if they address the needs of the business. In this session, it was first discussed how the strategic imperatives of innovation, cost reduction, and service quality shape organizations and their human resource management priorities. Then, several types of diversity initiatives were evaluated in the context of these priorities. Key features of alternative initiatives were considered in terms of how well they fit the HR priorities associated with the three strategic imperatives of innovation, cost reduction, and service quality. Finally, procedures that organizations can use to maximize the match between strategic imperatives and diversity were described.

Danelle Scarborough
San Diego's Commitment to Diversity

The City of San Diego is in the process of undergoing a change in its traditional values, norms, policies, and practices. The umbrella effort for this change is called, "The Diversity Commitment." Its goal is an environment where differences are valued and all 10,000 city employees are a productive part of a high-performing diverse team.

Decisions made in the initial stages of the program have set the city on a course of change that will touch every aspect of the organization. The strategies, challenges, risks, areas of resistance, joys, and insights involved in developing the city's readiness to undertake this meaningful diversity effort were presented and discussed.

Frederick A. Miller and Catherine S. Buntaine
Women and Men Working Together: A Partnership Paradigm

This interactive session explored the changing nature of woman-man work relationships. Beginning with an examination of the history of the bi-gender workplace, the common roles and scripts men and women use to define and shape their interactions at work were discussed. Topics explored included: how family roles and scripts influence workplace partnerships; dilemmas in cross-gender communications, conflict, and competition; managing sexual attraction and closeness; and differentiating "relationship" and "partnership."

The session concluded with some notions, generated by all, on the fundamentals of effective cross-gender partnering in the high-performing, inclusive workplace.

ROUND III OF CONCURRENT SESSIONS

Allen I. Kraut
Using Research to Frame and Act on Diversity Issues

This session covered *what to measure* in diversity research. It also stressed *how to do research* in a way that will predispose the results to be understood and used. Examples from recent studies in industry were used to illustrate these points.

The process of doing research is critical to later use of the findings. Some techniques were described to get key organizational players' initial involvement and continuing support, as well as their desire to use the final results.

Examples from actual practice included: How to develop a real sense of partnership with management; using conceptual models to tease out hidden assumptions and as a method of shaping the research issues; how to use others' research to educate and gain leverage; when and why to oversample critical groups; methods to gather believable data; and data analysis that reveals rather than obscures.

Also discussed were four basic measurement outcomes: reactions of employees to diversity and related change; knowledge of diversity and related initiatives; behavior on the job; and impact on organizational performance.

David A. Thomas
Mentoring, Diversity and Development in Organizations

The purpose of this workshop was to explore how mentoring dynamics are influenced by race and gender and the implications of this for organizations. The presentation also identified some of the factors that hamper formal mentoring programs, especially when they attempt to address diversity concerns. The information presented in this session was based on eight years of research and intervention in organizations. Participants were encouraged to share their own corporate experience attempting to link mentoring and diversity work.

Sunny Bradford and Ginger Lapid-Bogda
Leveraging Diverse Teams for High Performance

Organizations are relying increasingly on teams for achieving organizational goals; at the same time, organizations and their customer-bases are becoming more diverse. This combination of factors creates a need to understand how to create and sustain diverse work teams which are high performing. From experience with both consulting and studying diverse teams, in combination with an understanding of what contributes to team creativity and innovation, a model of diverse high-performing teams has been developed. This model examines three aspects of diverse teams: (1) what diverse high-performing teams look like, act like, etc.; (2) how diversity can be leveraged to enhance team performance; and (3) specific managerial skills which influence the successful functioning of diverse teams. The model focuses on the following team factors: leadership, vision, interpersonal skills, empowerment, innovation and problem solving, synergy, and feedback. In the context of working with diverse teams, there are increasingly effective ways to work with a variety of teams critical to diversity change efforts. These include diversity steering committees (councils, lead teams, etc.), employee networks, and senior management teams. Information about these types of groups and how they can be supported in their development is shared in this session.

Price M. Cobbs
Requirements of Diversity Leadership

Price M. Cobbs' session engaged the audience in thought and discussion about the requirements and process for leadership diversity. His model requires introspection, competencies, and skills at three levels: the personal, interpersonal, and the organizational.

At the personal level, the model involves leadership preparation where diversity is a core value and therefore helps frame thoughts, feelings, attitudes, and behavior. It means an examination of one's background to see where and how diversity is valued or what needs to change so it is valued.

At the interpersonal level, leadership diversity involves the ability to recognize delicate issues and hot buttons. Beyond competency and skill, it involves the courage to act on one's values and beliefs.

At the organizational level, Dr. Cobbs' model involves developing a strategy, a constellation of goals and the ability to model diversity behavior and lead an organization.

A goal of this session was for participants to think through the values underlying diversity and move past both dogma and political correctness.

Dawn M. Cross
Corning's Diversity Initiative

Dawn Cross reviewed the history and the rationale in order to provide a contextual background for Corning's diversity initiative. Since total quality is an essential part of the Corning culture, she described that linkage. She also discussed the range of Corning's diversity activities and initiatives, highlighting some of the more unique aspects of their endeavors.

Ms. Cross presented an evaluation of their efforts, assessing what's going well and what's not going so well. She made some brief comments about what they might do differently were they to begin their diversity efforts today: in other words, what they've learned about themselves and their effort.

This session concluded with a brief look at where Corning is heading with their effort in the next few years.

Appendix B
THE CONFERENCE AS A DATA-COLLECTION EFFORT

In addition to its role of stimulating action, the conference was viewed by the planning committee as a means to gather data from experts and professionals in the field of diversity on a number of controversial issues that are central in developing a diversity initiative. The conference polls and questionnaires served several purposes. The primary reason for the polls was to get participants to start thinking about issues and dilemmas related to developing diversity prior to attending the conference. During the conference, the data would be used to stimulate discussion about individuals' feelings and experience with different diversity practices after they had reviewed summaries of preconference responses.

Another purpose of the polls was to capture learnings from the conference and track opinions on diversity issues and practices during the course of the meeting; we also planned to use these data in the present conference report.

The preconference poll was administered to participants approximately six weeks prior to the conference. It consisted of three sections. Section A presented seven scenarios on diversity activities and implementation issues, with questions posed for each scenario. Data from the scenarios will not be reported in this appendix; some data from the scenarios have been used above in the text of this publication. Section B asked for background information on the participant and her or his organization with regard to progress on diversity efforts in the organization. The last section, C, asked the participant's opinion on issues often confronted in interventions. This included a ranking of effectiveness of practices for developing diversity and ratings on the appropriateness of outcomes as indicators of progress and on opinions about a variety of diversity interventions. Data from Section C of the preconference poll are reported in Tables 1-3.

At the end of the conference we asked participants to report their learnings from the meeting and their plans for next steps. This included two open-ended questions related to how the participant's learning at the conference influenced him or her to make changes or do things differently in his or her organization or personal life. For people responsible for implementing a diversity initiative or program in their organization, we asked how their learning will affect the next steps they take in their efforts.

The postconference poll was administered two months after the meeting. It repeated Section C of the preconference poll (opinions on issues confronted in interventions) as well as the two open-ended questions on learning and next steps. Quantitative data from the postconference poll are reported in Tables 4-6.

A copy of the preconference poll, postconference poll, and learning and next steps questionnaire follows, along with preconference and postconference poll data and tables.

Conference Prework

Section A: Scenarios

Please read the following seven scenarios and answer the questions posed for each.

Scenario 1

Jack argues that diversity activities are doomed until prejudice is addressed. He insists that diversity awareness training must be completed before other diversity practices are adopted. Jill counters that prejudice is so strong and pervasive that even a five-day training program will have little if any impact. She objects to spending money on training and instead recommends making changes in the performance evaluation and promotion systems.

Do you agree more with _____ Jack or _____ Jill. Why?

Do you think training is the most effective way to combat prejudice? Are there other strategies that you have found to be more effective?

Scenario 2

Your division has decided to begin a mentoring program for high-potential managers, including a number of nontraditionals. You are looking for upper-level managers who would be good mentors. You want a diverse group, in terms of demographics and functional areas of the business. You also want managers who are highly regarded and influence leaders. However, you know that these factors don't guarantee that these managers will be good mentors. What one or two other characteristics do you think would be critical for the individuals you select as mentors?

How would you determine whether someone had these characteristics (assessment tools or techniques, track record, etc.)?

How can managers be prepared to deal with problems that often arise in cross-sex and cross-race mentor relationships?

Scenario 3

As an independent consultant in this depressed economy, you have been requested by a large corporation to design and conduct a diversity training program for its 10,000 domestic employees. You already have a training design that you think will fit, and you are an accomplished trainer. What are the first steps you would take to ensure that your efforts are effective?

Scenario 4

You are the senior human-resource manager in your organization. Lately, several nontraditional managers have come to you to seek guidance about how to cope with the demands being made on them. They are exhausted in trying to meet extraordinary standards that they think are required to be seen as competent, and they feel torn between their career and their family and friends. They also feel lonely and isolated from their coworkers, somewhat adrift. They realize that changes are being made in the organization, but they are struggling now to survive and thrive.

What advice can you give them?

What specific tools or techniques are most helpful?

Scenario 5

You are president of a company. You have been thinking for the past few months that you should be doing something to develop diversity within the company, but you haven't yet decided what. Two officers of the black-employee group come to you requesting your support for a new development program for black supervisors in the company. The cost to the company would be quite reasonable, and there aren't any formal development programs at all in the company now. The officers remind you that there are only a handful of black managers in upper management. What do you do?

_____ Support the program. Explain your rationale and how you will support it.

_____ Reject their proposal. Explain why.

_____ Delay your decision until you have more information. Exactly what information do you need?

Scenario 6

The attrition rate among nontraditional managers has been rising, especially within the high-potential groups. From exit interviews you have learned that the main reason nontraditional managers have been leaving is that they feel their careers haven't been managed well. You realize that all of your organization's career planning practices have been developed for white men, and you worry that not enough attention has been given to the career development of nontraditionals.

Do you believe that career development models and tools based on white men apply to everyone? Explain.

What are the alternatives? That is, do you know of any useful tools or techniques that should be adopted?

Scenario 7

On September 18, an article in *The Wall Street Journal* noted that many corporations are changing the layoff policies to retain more nontraditional managers (who typically have less seniority). These corporations cite the need to compete for a demographically shifting customer base and to avoid job bias litigation. However, white men with more seniority feel cheated and victimized, and they fear there is no one looking out for them.

Do you believe that these policy changes are appropriate? ____ yes ____ no

Should diversity continue to be a priority when an organization is confronting economic troubles such as downsizing? ____ yes ____ no

What criteria should be used in deciding whom to lay off?

How would you handle backlash? That is, what would you do to respond to the perceptions of white men who feel they are not being fairly treated?

Section B: Background on you and your organization

What category best describes your role:
___ consultant   ___ researcher
___ internal HR professional/manager   ___ internal line manager
___ trainer   ___ other: _____

How many years have you been working on diversity issues? ____ years

Please answer the following questions only if you are responsible for or share responsibility for implementing a diversity initiative or program in your organization. Otherwise please skip this section and go to Section C.

How many years have you been employed at your organization? ____ years

At what step is your organization now in its diversity effort, and what is the next step?

Step 1: Internal Investigation ___ now ___ next
(Re)discover the problems, strengths, and priorities in your organization.

Step 2: Strengthen Top Management Commitment ___ now ___ next
Using data from Step 1 and other information, reinforce senior executives' inclination to take appropriate action.

Step 3: Choose and Develop Practices ___ now ___ next
(Re)create a balanced mix of practices to support strategic goals.

Step 4: Demand Results ___ now ___ next
Use statistical and qualitative measures to assess progress against key goals.

Step 5: Use Building Blocks ___ now ___next
Leverage strengths and successes to keep momentum going.

A year from now, where do you think your organization will be in terms of progress on developing diversity? ___ behind ___ about the same ___ way ahead

What was the first thing your organization did to develop diversity?

What has been the biggest achievement so far?

What was the biggest problem or dilemma you handled?

What is the biggest hurdle that lies ahead?

What factor or technique do you think contributed most to your success so far?

What indicators of success are you using?

Section C: Diversity issues

Please answer the following questions, which have to do with diversity issues often confronted in interventions.

Rank order (1 = most effective) the following practices in terms of their effectiveness for developing diversity in an organization.

    ___ Active intervention by top management
    ___ Recruiting nontraditional employees at non-managerial levels
    ___ Employee groups that advocate change
    ___ Consistent monitoring of statistical representation
    ___ Including diversity in performance evaluation goals and ratings
    ___ Including diversity in promotion decisions and criteria
    ___ Targeting nontraditional employees in the succession planning
         process
    ___ Diversity awareness training programs
    ___ Employee networks and support groups
    ___ Work-family policies
    ___ Other:

Rate the following in terms of their appropriateness as indicators of progress in developing diversity:

Very inappropriate 1, Inappropriate 2, Neutral 3, Appropriate 4,
Very appropriate 5

  ___ Statistical representation at different levels or functions
  ___ Turnover rates
  ___ Promotion rates
  ___ Representation in high-potential programs
  ___ Representation on replacement charts
  ___ Worker satisfaction
  ___ Differentials in compensation
  ___ Absenteeism
  ___ Complaint/grievance rates
  ___ Lawsuit
  ___ Representation in prestigious outside programs
  ___ Representation in training/development programs
  ___ Performance appraisal ratings
  ___ Employees completing diversity training
  ___ Number of diversity activities/programs
  ___ Inclusion of diversity in business strategy/policies
  ___ Other:

Rate the following according to a five-point scale from strongly agree to strongly disagree:

Strongly disagree 1, Disagree 2, Neutral 3, Agree 4, Strongly agree 5

1. ___ It's too hard to do work on diversity if you're a white man.

2. ___ We can use existing assessment tools and techniques to identify individuals best able to mentor nontraditional employees.

3. ___ It is impossible to create an environment of equal opportunity without having white men pay the price for past injustices.

4. ___ Organizations that hold managers accountable for statistical diversity goals have the best chance of achieving success in developing diversity.

5. ___ The problems typically arising from cross-sex and cross-race mentoring are so bad that it's not worth the risk.

6. ___ Racism and sexism have to be the primary targets in any diversity initiative.

7. ___ At this point, organizations need to do far more to accommodate diverse employees than vice versa.

8. ___ We can use existing assessment tools and techniques to identify individuals who are capable of developing diversity.

9. ___ Training is probably the most effective way to combat prejudice.

10. ___ It's just a matter of time until nontraditional employees reach senior management in many organizations.

11. ___ The reality in most organizations is that women can't have babies and an executive-level job.

12. ___ Diversity should remain a top priority for organizations regardless of economic conditions or other business hardships.

13. ___ Nontraditional employees need to take more responsibility for their own development and advancement.

14. ___ Prejudice is still the biggest advancement barrier for nontraditional managers.

15. ___ Organizations that don't tie diversity into a total quality management initiative are making a big mistake.

16. ___ It's a good idea to do diversity training even if it's clear that an organization does not want to undertake any other diversity activities.

17. ___ The same career development models and tools can be used with both nontraditional and traditional managers.

18. ___ Compliance with affirmative action guidelines remains a major problem in many diversity efforts.

19. ___ The criteria used to keep or promote employees need to reflect diversity goals.

20. ___ The work-family programs an organization offers represent a good way to assess its commitment to diversity.

21. ___ Since achieving diversity goals in organizations will take some time, nontraditional employees just need to accept things as they are for a while longer.

22. ___ Since women and people of color have been at a disadvantage for so long, programs exclusively for them need to be provided.

Learning and Next Steps

We hope that this conference will have a lasting impact on how you develop diversity. Please describe what you plan to do differently as a result of your learning at this conference.

If you are responsible for or share responsibility for implementing a diversity initiative or program in your organization, use the following space to note how your learning here will impact the next steps you take in this effort.

Whether or not you are personally involved in a diversity initiative, use the following space to describe what you will do differently in your work (such as new diversity tools, different research topics or methods, different evaluation criteria) or in your life.

Postconference Poll

We are interested in tracking how opinions on diversity issues and practices may have changed during the course of the conference. This will play a significant role in the report we write on the conference. To do this, we plan to compare your prework with this questionnaire. Therefore we ask that you put your name on the form so that we can match surveys. Your responses to the prework are confidential and will only be seen by those of us working on the survey.

Please answer the following questions, which have to do with diversity issues often confronted in interventions.

Rank order (1 = most effective) the following practices in terms of their effectiveness for developing diversity in an organization.

_____ Active intervention by top management
_____ Recruiting nontraditional employees at non-managerial levels
_____ Employee groups that advocate change
_____ Consistent monitoring of statistical representation
_____ Including diversity in performance evaluation goals and ratings
_____ Including diversity in promotion decisions and criteria
_____ Targeting nontraditional employees in the succession planning process
_____ Diversity awareness training programs
_____ Employee networks and support groups
_____ Work-family policies
_____ Other:

Rate the following in terms of their appropriateness as indicators of progress in developing diversity:

Very inappropriate 1, Inappropriate 2, Neutral 3, Appropriate 4,
Very appropriate 5

_____ Statistical representation at different levels or functions
_____ Turnover rates
_____ Promotion rates
_____ Representation in high-potential programs
_____ Representation on replacement charts
_____ Worker satisfaction
_____ Differentials in compensation
_____ Absenteeism
_____ Complaint/grievance rates
_____ Lawsuit

___ Representation in prestigious outside programs
___ Representation in training/development programs
___ Performance appraisal ratings
___ Employees completing diversity training
___ Number of diversity activities/programs
___ Inclusion of diversity in business strategy/policies
___ Other:

Rate the following according to a five-point scale from strongly agree to strongly disagree:

Strongly disagree 1, Disagree 2, Neutral 3, Agree 4, Strongly agree 5

1. ___ It's too hard to do work on diversity if you're a white man.

2. ___ We can use existing assessment tools and techniques to identify individuals best able to mentor nontraditional employees.

3. ___ It is impossible to create an environment of equal opportunity without having white men pay the price for past injustices.

4. ___ Organizations that hold managers accountable for statistical diversity goals have the best chance of achieving success in developing diversity.

5. ___ The problems typically arising from cross-sex and cross-race mentoring are so bad that it's not worth the risk.

6. ___ Racism and sexism have to be the primary targets in any diversity initiative.

7. ___ At this point, organizations need to do far more to accommodate diverse employees than vice versa.

8. ___ We can use existing assessment tools and techniques to identify individuals who are capable of developing diversity.

9. ___ Training is probably the most effective way to combat prejudice.

10. ___ It's just a matter of time until nontraditional employees reach senior management in many organizations.

11. ___ The reality in most organizations is that women can't have babies and an executive-level job.

12. ___ Diversity should remain a top priority for organizations regardless of economic conditions or other business hardships.

13. ___ Nontraditional employees need to take more responsibility for their own development and advancement.

14. ___ Prejudice is still the biggest advancement barrier for nontraditional managers.

15. ___ Organizations that don't tie diversity into a total quality management initiative are making a big mistake.

16. ___ It's a good idea to do diversity training even if it's clear that an organization does not want to undertake any other diversity activities.

17. ___ The same career development models and tools can be used with both nontraditional and traditional managers.

18. ___ Compliance with affirmative action guidelines remains a major problem in many diversity efforts.

19. ___ The criteria used to keep or promote employees need to reflect diversity goals.

20. ___ The work-family programs an organization offers represent a good way to assess its commitment to diversity.

21. ___ Since achieving diversity goals in organizations will take some time, nontraditional employees just need to accept things as they are for a while longer.

22. ___ Since women and people of color have been at a disadvantage for so long, programs exclusively for them need to be provided.

We hope that the conference had an impact on how you develop diversity. Please indicate what you have done differently as a result of your learning at this conference.

If you are responsible for or share responsibility for implementing a diversity initiative or program in your organization, please indicate how your learning at the conference has influenced your handling of this responsibility.

Whether or not you are personally involved in a diversity initiative, use the following space to describe what you have done differently in your work or personal life as a result of the conference.

Preconference and Postconference Poll Data

One hundred four participants completed the preconference poll. The background section of the survey asked participants about their roles in the organization. The majority of respondents were internal human-resource professionals or managers (38%), with the remainder describing their role as consultants (17%), trainers (16%), researchers (13%), and line managers (2%). A number of respondents selected the "other" category, and listed roles such as affirmative action administrator, professor, student, and organizational effectiveness supervisor. Fifty-one percent of the respondents are responsible or share responsibility for implementing a diversity initiative or program in their organization.

Fifty-eight participants completed the postconference poll. Fifty-two of these respondents were included in the preconference poll sample.

Tables 1 (preconference poll) and 4 (postconference poll) report means and percentages from the rank ordering of a list of ten practices in terms of their effectiveness for developing diversity. The ten practices listed were the ten "best practices" found to be most important in the research for *The New Leaders*.

Tables 2 (preconference poll) and 5 (postconference poll) summarize participants' opinions on the appropriateness (on a scale of 1 to 5, with 5 being "very appropriate") of outcomes as measures of progress in developing diversity. The outcomes as measures of progress were based on suggestions made by managers interviewed in *The New Leaders* research. Means and percentages of rating options are listed for each item.

Means and percentages of rating options for the final twenty-two questions of the pre- and postconference polls, reported in Tables 3 and 6, reflect participants' agreement (on a scale of 1 to 5, with 5 being "strongly agree") with a variety of statements. Some of these statements pertain to issues raised in the scenarios.

TABLE 1

PRECONFERENCE POLL: Ranking of Effectiveness of Practices

Mean	Item	Ranking Percentage										
		1	2	3	4	5	6	7	8	9	10	11
1.57	Active intervention by top management	80.2	9.9	3.0	1.0	2.0	0	0	1.0	3.0	0	0
6.97	Recruiting nontraditional employees at non-managerial levels	0	4.1	6.2	9.3	10.3	10.3	14.4	9.3	17.5	17.5	1.0
6.68	Employee groups that advocate change	5.1	10.1	4.0	7.1	7.1	7.1	9.1	13.1	18.2	19.2	0
6.92	Consistent monitoring of statistical representation	0	3.1	8.2	6.2	11.3	10.3	13.4	18.6	13.4	15.5	0
4.10	Including diversity in performance evaluation goals and ratings	6.1	25.3	18.2	15.2	9.1	10.1	5.1	6.1	2.0	3.0	0
4.56	Including diversity in promotion decisions and criteria	6.3	10.4	16.7	18.8	17.7	14.6	4.2	5.2	5.2	1.0	0
4.57	Targeting nontraditional employees in the succession planning process	6.1	9.1	17.2	25.3	16.2	6.1	8.1	5.1	5.1	2.0	0
4.25	Diversity awareness training programs	8.0	23.0	17.0	9.0	10.0	14.0	7.0	9.0	1.0	2.0	0
6.18	Employee networks and support groups	1.0	10.2	12.2	5.1	6.1	12.2	17.3	14.3	14.3	7.1	0
6.94	Work-family policies	3.1	5.2	6.2	3.1	5.2	9.3	19.6	14.4	14.4	18.6	0
3.78	Other	33.3	22.2	0	11.1	0	22.2	0	0	0	0	11.1

Participants rank ordered the items 1 to 11, where 1 = most effective and 11 = least effective.

TABLE 2
PRECONFERENCE POLL: Appropriateness of Indicators of Progress

Mean	Item	Rating Percentage				
		1	2	3	4	5
4.48	Statistical representation at different levels or functions	0	1.9	1.9	42.3	53.8
4.21	Turnover rates	1.9	4.9	6.8	42.7	43.7
4.34	Promotion rates	1.9	0	6.8	44.7	46.6
4.42	Representation in high-potential programs	1.9	0	1.9	46.2	50.0
4.09	Representation on replacement charts	0	2.0	21.2	42.4	34.3
4.16	Worker satisfaction	2.0	1.0	14.9	43.6	38.6
3.91	Differentials in compensation	2.9	11.8	8.8	44.1	32.4
3.24	Absenteeism	5.1	15.2	39.4	31.3	9.1
3.61	Complaint/grievance rates	2.9	9.7	23.3	51.5	12.6
3.34	Lawsuits	3.0	18.8	22.8	52.5	3.0
3.63	Representation in prestigious outside programs	1.0	8.1	35.4	38.4	17.2
4.03	Representation in training/development programs	2.0	4.0	14.1	48.5	31.3
3.80	Performance appraisal ratings	4.0	8.9	18.8	39.6	28.7
3.85	Employees completing diversity training	2.0	2.0	25.5	50.0	20.6
3.65	Number of diversity activities/programs	1.9	3.9	35.0	45.6	13.6
4.77	Inclusion of diversity in business strategy/policies	1.0	0	0	18.6	80.4
4.71	Other:_____	0	0	0	28.6	71.4

Participants rated items on a scale of 1 to 5, where 1 = Very inappropriate, 2 = Inappropriate, 3 = Neutral, 4 = Appropriate, and 5 = Very appropriate.

TABLE 3
PRECONFERENCE POLL: Opinions About Diversity Interventions

Mean	Item	Rating Percentage				
		1	2	3	4	5
1.57	It's too hard to do work on diversity if you're a white man.	65.4	24.0	2.9	3.8	3.8
2.63	We can use existing assessment tools and techniques to identify individuals best able to mentor non-traditional employees.	4.9	46.6	31.1	15.5	1.9
2.23	It is impossible to create an environment of equal opportunity without having white men pay the price for past injustices.	25.5	43.1	15.7	14.7	1.0
3.54	Organizations that hold managers accountable for statistical diversity goals have the best chance of achieving success in developing diversity.	2.9	18.4	19.4	39.8	19.4
1.47	The problems typically arising from cross-sex and cross-race mentoring are so bad that it's not worth the risk.	59.6	34.6	4.8	1.0	0
3.33	Racism and sexism have to be the primary targets in any diversity initiative.	7.7	27.9	8.7	35.6	20.2
3.86	At this point, organizations need to do far more to accommodate diverse employees than vice versa.	2.9	14.7	8.8	40.2	33.3
2.77	We can use existing assessment tools and techniques to identify individuals who are capable of developing diversity.	4.0	36.6	39.6	17.8	2.0
2.91	Training is probably the most effective way to combat prejudice.	4.9	36.9	27.2	24.3	6.8
2.20	It's just a matter of time until nontraditional employees reach senior management in many organizations.	24.0	51.0	9.6	11.5	3.8
2.78	The reality in most organizations is that women can't have babies and an executive-level job.	23.1	26.9	6.7	35.6	7.7
4.46	Diversity should remain a top priority for organizations regardless of economic conditions or other business hardships.	0	1.0	4.8	41.3	52.9

Participants rated items on a scale of 1 to 5, where 1 = Strongly disagree, 2 = Disagree, 3 = Neutral, 4 = Agree, and 5 = Strongly agree.

(continued)

TABLE 3 (cont.)
PRECONFERENCE POLL: Opinions About Diversity Interventions

Mean	Item	Rating Percentage				
		1	2	3	4	5
3.61	Nontraditional employees need to take more responsibility for their own development and advancement.	1.0	11.7	23.3	53.4	10.7
3.99	Prejudice is still the biggest advancement barrier for nontraditional managers.	1.0	10.7	6.8	51.5	30.1
4.03	Organizations that don't tie diversity into a total quality management initiative are making a big mistake.	1.0	3.9	17.5	46.6	31.1
2.64	It's a good idea to do diversity training even if it's clear that an organization does not want to undertake any other diversity activities.	19.2	37.5	10.6	25.0	7.7
2.40	The same career development models and tools can be used with both nontraditional and traditional managers.	11.8	53.9	18.6	13.7	2.0
3.24	Compliance with affirmative action guidelines remains a major problem in many diversity efforts.	3.1	20.4	31.6	38.8	6.1
4.20	The criteria used to keep or promote employees need to reflect diversity goals.	0	6.9	4.9	50.0	38.2
3.64	The work-family programs an organization offers represent a good way to assess its commitment to diversity.	1.0	15.5	18.4	48.5	16.5
1.90	Since achieving diversity goals in organizations will take some time, nontraditional employees just need to accept things as they are for a while longer.	29.8	58.7	5.8	2.9	2.9
3.33	Some women and people of color have been at a disadvantage for so long, programs exclusively for them need to be provided.	3.8	26.9	14.4	42.3	12.5

Participants rated items on a scale of 1 to 5, where 1 = Strongly disagree, 2 = Disagree, 3 = Neutral, 4 = Agree, and 5 = Strongly agree.

TABLE 4
POSTCONFERENCE POLL: Ranking of Effectiveness of Practices

Mean	Item	Ranking Percentage										
		1	2	3	4	5	6	7	8	9	10	11
1.19	Active intervention by top management	91.4	5.2	1.7	0	0	0	1.7.	0	0	0	0
7.14	Recruiting nontraditional employees at non-managerial levels	0	6.9	6.9	6.9	8.6	10.3	5.2	12.1	19.0	22.4	1.7
6.67	Employee groups that advocate change	0	12.1	8.6	3.4	6.9	3.4	15.5	22.4	15.5	12.1	0
6.14	Consistent monitoring of statistical representation	0	6.9	6.9	6.9	17.2	15.5	20.7	12.1	6.9	6.9	0
3.71	Including diversity in performance evaluation goals and ratings	1.7	25.9	32.8	15.5	8.6	5.2	5.2	1.7	1.7	1.7	0
4.43	Including diversity in promotion decisions and criteria	0	10.3	20.7	36.2	10.3	6.9	5.2	6.9	3.4	0	0
4.88	Targeting nontraditional employees in the succession planning process	0	12.1	10.3	17.2	22.4	24.1	8.6	1.7	1.7	1.7	0
5.41	Diversity awareness training programs	1.7	19.0	5.2	1.7	15.5	20.7	22.4	6.9	3.4	3.4	0
7.59	Employee networks and support groups	0	0	5.2	10.3	1.7	6.9	12.1	24.1	22.4	17.2	0
8.28	Work-family policies	1.7	0	1.7	1.7	8.6	6.9	5.2	12.1	25.9	34.5	1.7
1.50	Other _____	50.0	50.0	0	0	0	0	0	0	0	0	0

Participants rank ordered the items 1 to 11, where 1 = most effective and 11 = least effective.

TABLE 5

POSTCONFERENCE POLL: Appropriateness of Indicators of Progress

Mean	Item	Rating Percentage				
		1	2	3	4	5
4.66	Statistical representation at different levels or functions	0	0	0	33.9	66.1
4.30	Turnover rates	0	1.8	3.6	57.1	37.5
4.50	Promotion rates	0	3.6	0	39.3	57.1
4.36	Representation in high-potential programs	0	3.6	3.6	46.4	46.4
4.24	Representation on replacement charts	0	0	12.7	50.9	36.4
3.93	Worker satisfaction	0	0	23.2	60.7	16.1
3.98	Differentials in compensation	1.8	5.4	14.3	50.0	28.6
3.29	Absenteeism	1.8	10.7	50.0	32.1	5.4
3.63	Complaint/grievance rates	0	7.1	33.9	48.2	10.7
3.54	Lawsuits	1.8	10.7	33.9	39.3	14.3
3.63	Representation in prestigious outside programs	0	8.9	33.9	42.9	14.3
4.00	Representation in training/development programs	0	3.6	17.9	53.6	25.0
3.91	Performance appraisal ratings	1.8	5.4	21.4	42.9	28.6
3.82	Employees completing diversity training	0	3.6	19.6	67.9	8.9
3.70	Number of diversity activities/programs	0	7.1	25.0	58.9	8.9
4.79	Inclusion of diversity in business strategy/policies	0	0	5.4	10.7	83.9
5.00	Other:_____	0	0	0	0	100

Participants rated items on a scale of 1 to 5, where 1 = Very inappropriate, 2 = Inappropriate,
3 = Neutral, 4 = Appropriate, and 5 = Very appropriate.

TABLE 6
POSTCONFERENCE POLL: Opinions About Diversity Interventions

Mean	Item	Rating Percentage				
		1	2	3	4	5
1.53	It's too hard to do work on diversity if you're a white man.	56.9	36.2	5.2	0	1.7
2.74	We can use existing assessment tools and techniques to identify individuals best able to mentor non-traditional employees.	3.4	48.3	19.0	29.3	0
2.50	It is impossible to create an environment of equal opportunity without having white men pay the price for past injustices.	22.4	37.9	12.1	22.4	5.2
3.88	Organizations that hold managers accountable for statistical diversity goals have the best chance of achieving success in developing diversity.	0	12.1	13.8	48.3	25.9
1.69	The problems typically arising from cross-sex and cross-race mentoring are so bad that it's not worth the risk.	37.9	55.2	6.9	0	0
3.81	Racism and sexism have to be the primary targets in any diversity initiative.	1.7	19.0	1.7	51.7	25.9
3.91	At this point, organizations need to do far more to accommodate diverse employees than vice versa.	1.7	10.3	17.2	36.2	34.5
2.75	We can use existing assessment tools and techniques to identify individuals who are capable of developing diversity.	1.8	47.4	26.3	22.8	1.8
2.88	Training is probably the most effective way to combat prejudice.	5.2	39.7	20.7	31.0	3.4
2.10	It's just a matter of time until nontraditional employees reach senior management in many organizations.	27.6	51.7	6.9	10.3	3.4
2.76	The reality in most organizations is that women can't have babies and an executive-level job.	22.4	29.3	6.9	32.8	8.6
4.43	Diversity should remain a top priority for organizations regardless of economic conditions or other business hardships.	0	3.4	5.2	36.2	55.2

Participants rated items on a scale of 1 to 5, where 1 = Strongly disagree, 2 = Disagree, 3 = Neutral, 4 = Agree, and 5 = Strongly agree.

(continued)

TABLE 6 (cont.)
POSTCONFERENCE POLL: Opinions About Diversity Interventions

Mean	Item	Rating Percentage				
		1	2	3	4	5
3.66	Nontraditional employees need to take more responsibility for their own development and advancement.	0	8.6	25.9	56.9	8.6
4.43	Prejudice is still the biggest advancement barrier for nontraditional managers.	0	3.4	6.9	32.8	56.9
4.07	Organizations that don't tie diversity into a total quality management initiative are making a big mistake.	3.4	1.7	12.1	50.0	32.8
2.48	It's a good idea to do diversity training even if it's clear that an organization does not want to undertake any other diversity activities.	16.1	44.6	17.9	17.9	3.6
2.39	The same career development models and tools can be used with both nontraditional and traditional managers.	10.5	50.9	28.1	10.5	0
3.26	Compliance with affirmative action guidelines remains a major problem in many diversity efforts.	1.8	19.3	31.6	45.6	1.8
4.44	The criteria used to keep or promote employees need to reflect diversity goals.	0	0	5.3	45.6	49.1
3.75	The work-family programs an organization offers represent a good way to assess its commitment to diversity.	0	10.5	17.5	57.9	14.0
1.77	Since achieving diversity goals in organizations will take some time, nontraditional employees just need to accept things as they are for a while longer.	31.6	61.4	5.3	1.8	0
3.33	Some women and people of color have been at a disadvantage for so long, programs exclusively for them need to be provided.	5.3	21.1	17.5	47.4	8.8

Participants rated items on a scale of 1 to 5, where 1 = Strongly disagree, 2 = Disagree, 3 = Neutral, 4 = Agree, and 5 = Strongly agree.

CENTER FOR CREATIVE LEADERSHIP PUBLICATIONS

SELECTED REPORTS:

Beyond Work-Family Programs J.R. Kofodimos (1995, Stock #167) $25.00

CEO Selection: A Street-Smart Review G.P. Hollenbeck (1994, Stock #164) $25.00

Character Shifts: The Challenge of Improving Executive Performance Through Personal Growth R.E. Kaplan (1990, Stock #143) $30.00

Coping With an Intolerable Boss M.M. Lombardo & M.W. McCall, Jr. (1984, Stock #305) $10.00

The Creative Opportunists: Conversations with the CEOs of Small Businesses
J.S. Bruce (1992, Stock #316) $12.00

Creativity in the R&D Laboratory T.M. Amabile & S.S. Gryskiewicz (1987, Stock #130) $12.00

The Dynamics of Management Derailment M.M. Lombardo & C.D. McCauley (1988, Stock #134) $12.00

Eighty-eight Assignments for Development in Place: Enhancing the Developmental Challenge of Existing Jobs M.M. Lombardo & R.W. Eichinger (1989, Stock #136) $15.00

Enhancing 360-degree Feedback for Senior Executives: How to Maximize the Benefits and Minimize the Risks R.E. Kaplan & C.J. Palus (1994, Stock #160) $15.00

An Evaluation of the Outcomes of a Leadership Development Program C.D. McCauley & M.W. Hughes-James (1994, Stock #163) $35.00

The Expansive Executive (Second Edition) R.E. Kaplan (1991, Stock #147) $25.00

Feedback to Managers, Volume I: A Guide to Evaluating Multi-rater Feedback Instruments E.Van Velsor & J. Brittain Leslie (1991, Stock #149) $20.00

Feedback to Managers, Volume II: A Review and Comparison of Sixteen Multi-rater Feedback Instruments E. Van Velsor & J. Brittain Leslie (1991, Stock #150).................................... $80.00

Gender Differences in the Development of Managers: How Women Managers Learn From Experience E. Van Velsor & M. W. Hughes (1990, Stock #145) $35.00

High Hurdles: The Challenge of Executive Self-Development R.E. Kaplan, W.H. Drath, & J.R. Kofodimos (1985, Stock #125) $15.00

The Intuitive Pragmatists: Conversations with Chief Executive Officers J.S. Bruce (1986, Stock #310) $12.00

Key Events in Executives' Lives E.H. Lindsey, V. Homes, & M.W. McCall, Jr. (1987, Stock #132) $65.00

Leadership for Turbulent Times L.R. Sayles (1995, Stock #325) $20.00

Learning How to Learn From Experience: Impact of Stress and Coping K.A. Bunker & A.D. Webb (1992, Stock #154) $30.00

Making Common Sense: Leadership as Meaning-making in a Community of Practice W.H. Drath & C.J. Palus (1994, Stock #156) $15.00

Off the Track: Why and How Successful Executives Get Derailed M.W. McCall, Jr., & M.M. Lombardo (1983, Stock #121) $10.00

Preventing Derailment: What To Do Before It's Too Late M.M. Lombardo & R.W. Eichinger (1989, Stock #138) $25.00

Readers' Choice: A Decade of *Issues & Observations* W.H. Drath, Editor (1990, Stock #314) $15.00

The Realities of Management Promotion M.N. Ruderman & P.J. Ohlott (1994, Stock #157) $20.00

Redefining What's Essential to Business Performance: Pathways to Productivity, Quality, and Service L.R. Sayles (1990, Stock #142) $20.00

Training for Action: A New Approach to Executive Development R.M. Burnside & V.A. Guthrie (1992, Stock #153) $15.00

Traps and Pitfalls in the Judgment of Executive Potential M.N. Ruderman & P.J. Ohlott (1990, Stock #141) $20.00

Twenty-two Ways to Develop Leadership in Staff Managers R.W. Eichinger & M.M. Lombardo (1990, Stock #144) $15.00

Understanding Executive Performance: A Life-Story Perspective C.J. Palus, W. Nasby, & R.D. Easton (1991, Stock #148) $20.00

Upward-communication Programs in American Industry A.I. Kraut & F.H. Freeman (1992, Stock #152) $30.00

Why Executives Lose Their Balance J.R. Kofodimos (1989, Stock #137) $20.00

Why Managers Have Trouble Empowering: A Theoretical Perspective Based on Concepts of Adult Development W.H. Drath (1993, Stock #155) $15.00

SELECTED BOOKS:

Balancing Act: How Managers Can Integrate Successful Careers and Fulfilling Personal Lives
J.R. Kofodimos (1993, Stock #247) $27.00
Beyond Ambition: How Driven Managers Can Lead Better and Live Better R.E. Kaplan,
W.H. Drath, & J.R. Kofodimos (1991, Stock #227) $29.95
Breaking the Glass Ceiling: Can Women Reach the Top of America's Largest Corporations?
(Updated Edition) A.M. Morrison, R.P. White, & E. Van Velsor (1992, Stock #236) $19.95
Choosing to Lead K.E. Clark & M.B. Clark (1994, Stock #249) $35.00
Developing Diversity in Organizations: A Digest of Selected Literature A.M. Morrison &
K.M. Crabtree (1992, Stock #317) $25.00
Discovering Creativity: Proceedings of the 1992 International Creativity and Innovation
Networking Conference S.S. Gryskiewicz (Ed.) (1993, Stock #319) $30.00
Executive Selection: A Look at What We Know and What We Need to Know
D.L. DeVries (1993, Stock #321) $20.00
Healing the Wounds: Overcoming the Trauma of Layoffs and Revitalizing Downsized
Organizations D.M. Noer (1993, Stock #245) $26.00
If I'm In Charge Here, Why Is Everybody Laughing? D.P. Campbell (1980, Stock #205) $9.40
If You Don't Know Where You're Going You'll Probably End Up Somewhere Else
D.P. Campbell (1974, Stock #203) $8.95
Impact of Leadership K.E. Clark, M.B. Clark, & D.P. Campbell (Eds.) (1992, Stock #235) $59.50
Inklings: Collected Columns on Leadership and Creativity D.P. Campbell (1992, Stock #233) $15.00
Leadership Education 1994-1995: A Source Book F.H. Freeman, K.B. Knott, &
M.K. Schwartz (Eds.) (1994, Stock #322) $59.00
Leadership: Enhancing the Lessons of Experience R.L. Hughes, R.C. Ginnett, & G.J. Curphy
(1992, Stock #246) $40.95
The Lessons of Experience: How Successful Executives Develop on the Job M.W. McCall, Jr.,
M.M. Lombardo, & A.M. Morrison (1988, Stock #211) $22.95
Making Diversity Happen: Controversies and Solutions A.M. Morrison, M.N. Ruderman, &
M. Hughes-James (1993, Stock #320) $25.00
Measures of Leadership K.E. Clark & M.B. Clark (Eds.) (1990, Stock #215) $59.50
The New Leaders: Guidelines on Leadership Diversity in America A.M. Morrison
(1992, Stock #238) $29.00
Performance Appraisal on the Line D.L. DeVries, A.M. Morrison, S.L. Shullman, &
M.L. Gerlach (1981, Stock #206) $15.00
Readings in Innovation S.S. Gryskiewicz & D.A. Hills (Eds.) (1992, Stock #240) $25.00
Take the Road to Creativity and Get Off Your Dead End D.P. Campbell (1977, Stock #204) $8.95
Whatever It Takes: The Realities of Managerial Decision Making (Second Edition)
M.W. McCall, Jr., & R.E. Kaplan (1990, Stock #218) $30.40
The Working Leader: The Triumph of High Performance Over Conventional Management
Principles L.R. Sayles (1993, Stock #243) $24.95

SPECIAL PACKAGES:

Conversations with CEOs (includes 310 & 316) $16.00
Development & Derailment (includes 136, 138, & 144) $30.00
The Diversity Collection (includes 145, 236, 238, 317, & 320) $85.00
Executive Selection Package (includes 141, 321, & 157) $32.00
Feedback to Managers: Volumes I & II (includes 149 & 150) $85.00
Personal Growth, Taking Charge, and Enhancing Creativity (includes 203, 204, & 205) $20.00

Discounts are available. Please write for a comprehensive Publication & Products Catalog. Address
your request to: Publication, Center for Creative Leadership, P.O. Box 26300, Greensboro, NC
27438-6300, 910-545-2805, or fax to 910-545-3221. All prices subject to change.

ORDER FORM

Name _____ Title _____

Organization _____

Mailing Address_____
(street address required for mailing)

City/State/Zip _____

Telephone _____ FAX _____
(telephone number required for UPS mailing)

Quantity	Stock No.	Title	Unit Cost	Amount

Subtotal	
Shipping and Handling (add 6% of subtotal with a $4.00 minimum; add 40% on all international shipping)	
All NC Residents add 6% sales tax	
TOTAL	

METHOD OF PAYMENT

❏ Check or money order enclosed (payable to Center for Creative Leadership).

❏ Purchase Order No. _____ (Must be accompanied by this form.)

❏ Charge my order, plus shipping, to my credit card:
    ❏ American Express ❏ Discover ❏ MasterCard ❏ VISA

ACCOUNT NUMBER: _____ EXPIRATION DATE: MO. ____ YR. ____

NAME OF ISSUING BANK: _____

SIGNATURE _____

❏ Please put me on your mailing list.
❏ Please send me the Center's quarterly newsletter, *Issues & Observations*.

Publication • Center for Creative Leadership • P.O. Box 26300
Greensboro, NC 27438-6300
910-545-2805 • FAX 910-545-3221

0595

Client Priority Code: R

fold here

CENTER FOR CREATIVE LEADERSHIP
PUBLICATION
P.O. Box 26300
Greensboro, NC 27438-6300